❖《《❖《❖《 **HONORÉ** De **BALZAC** 》❖》❖》❖》❖

MASTERS OF WORLD LITERATURE

MASTERS OF WORLD LITERATURE SERIES

LOUIS KRONENBERGER, GENERAL EDITOR

Honoré de Balzac

by E. J. Oliver

The Macmillan Company, New York
Collier-Macmillan Limited, London

18127

First Printing

The Macmillan Company, New York
Collier-Macmillan Canada, Ltd., Toronto, Ontario

Library of Congress catalog card number: 64-25418

Printed in the United States of America

DESIGNED BY RONALD FARBER

◆((◆((◆((CONTENTS)◆)◆)◆)◆

◄‹‹‹‹‹‹‹ **HONORÉ** DE **BALZAC** ›››››

Images of Balzac

A LARGE HEAD, neck finely moulded to the trunk, strong shoulders, a powerfully built figure—that is the first impression of Balzac. Rodin tried to create an image of this power, tried again and again, in a nude figure of Balzac, in another shapeless monster, finally in a great head rising from a primitive block—his monastic robe—the statue which today stands at the juncture of the boulevards Raspail and Montparnasse, above Paris though not in the quarter where Rastignac issued his famous challenge: "*A nous deux maintenant*—I'm ready for you now."

Rodin's is the best figure available, though one on the scale of Michelangelo's David was required, for Balzac had many qualities which belonged more to the Renaissance than to the nineteenth century, and his work sometimes has the grasp of the "terrible" Michelangelo. Yet it is important not to exaggerate the height of this figure, for as one of his heroes Balzac had "the medium height of all great men." He was referring to Napoleon in this, but also to himself, as so often when he wrote of Napoleon, determined, so he said, to complete with the pen what he had begun with the sword. Barbey d'Aurevilly, his most fervent admirer, who never even dared to talk to Balzac when they were together in

the Passy horse-bus, went further than this to declare
that he was "a literary Bonaparte who never had to
adbicate nor lose the Battle of Waterloo."

At least he was an impressive figure, Napoleonic—yet
this is precisely the point at which Balzac criticism runs
into the first difficulties, and his admirers become angry
or embarrassed by smiles and mockery. Napoleon was
a great man, certainly, but one who—at least after his
fall—has always invited caricature, and delusions of
grandeur have made him the perfect model for all
madmen, so that his name today, though not diminished
in history, bulks large in the case histories of psychology.
Balzac too was often caricatured even in his lifetime:
one cartoon shows him gaily riding on a swing made
from the long hair of women on his right and left, borne
to triumph by the "women of thirty" whom he described
with such sympathy, while more women acclaim him in
the background. He was Napoleonic, but he was also a
figure of fun, and when at the height of his fame he
applied, not for the first time, for admission to the French
Academy, he received only two votes, those of Hugo and
Lamartine. Yet there was some justice in that, as they
were the only two worthy to hold a candle to his greater
light.

He was a powerful figure, but an awkward one, and
those who knew him best more often noted his exuberant
or childish traits than the dignity of a great man. He
described himself more than once in his work, in the
figure of Benassis, the country doctor, when he was
anxious to impress Madame de Castries, or in Albert
Savarus when he wanted to reassure Madame Hanska.
Both were men with the strength of passion and the
marks of suffering in their faces, while Savarus had his
own fine neck which he bared with the defiance of a man
facing the guillotine. This noble appearance was joined
to the physique of a peasant, and some thought he would

have looked more at home behind a butcher's apron in a provincial town, though when success came he dressed as a dandy, and carried a cane with an exotically carved ivory handle, on which Delphine Gay based a novel, *La Canne de M. de Balzac.*

The power is evident enough in the fifty-one years of the short life between 1799 and 1850, in less than twenty years of which he wrote more than ninety works, many of them long. Nor is the intellect in question: the philosopher Alain declared that he had learned more from Balzac than from philosophers and critics. Yet when his sister Laure de Surville tried to recall early signs of intelligence or genius in his childhood, she had to admit that what had always impressed her most was his good nature. George Sand, with her greater experience of men, spoke of his unfailing good humour. Lamartine said that it was "impossible for him not to be good-natured . . . impossible not to share his joyousness." All observers noted his vivacity, the sparkle and joy in his brown eyes, his childish eagerness.

So the powerful build and Napoleonic image have to be qualified by this expression of the eyes beyond the reach of a sculptor, difficult for any artist, though a glitter at least shows in the sketch by David d'Angers above the strong nose to which Balzac drew his attention: "My nose is a world in itself."

Evidently the eyes expressed the Rabelaisian humour of his *Contes drolatiques*, modelled on Rabelais himself, which are still issued in the most lurid of paperbacks—an oddity from the author of *Séraphita*, which was modelled on the mysticism of Swedenborg. It is a question whether Balzac disconcerts more by his grossness or by his sublimity.

At least he still disconcerts, for if he continues to capture his readers, some of the ridicule and the amazement—and some of the misunderstanding—which he aroused in Paris in his time is still to be observed in a number of his critics, who find too much of his own exaggeration in his works. For this reason it is more convenient to discover what sort of man he was and the figure he cut in the world before any judgment on his writings, as it is usually affection for him which brings enjoyment to reading Balzac and antipathy for his character which depreciates his work.

Some have similar reactions to Henry James, for whom Balzac was "first and foremost." Their characters were at opposite poles, but both provoke the same contrast between those who, in fondness and amusement at their peculiar traits, respect them as masters, and those who quite miss their enchantment, even finding them difficult to read. In both, distinct from other great writers on whom criticism is more uniform, there is a quality which attracts some no less than it repels others. Both too produced a great body of work which is never excessive to their admirers, because it is stamped throughout with their own extraordinary personalities.

There is a further resemblance in that both Balzac and Henry James create for some an atmosphere of serenity in which others find an image of desolation. To Mr. Graham Greene, Henry James is above all the analyst of disillusion, of innocence cruelly deceived, though more see in him the most serene of masters, and even Conrad in his Slav melancholy agreed that "his mankind is delightful." So to M. Claude Mauriac and to those who complain that *La Comédie humaine* should really be called a tragedy, Balzac is the most ruthless of pessimists, though another French critic has asserted that his whole work is a chant of joy, its delight never obscured by the grimness of the subject matter—and Balzac's own joyousness can no more be questioned than the charm of Henry James.

Balzac himself maintained in the original preface to *La Peau de chagrin* that a man may be wholly different from his work, though this was largely to disclaim the cynicism of his *Physiologie du mariage* which had appeared two years before. In *Facino Cane* he referred to the extraordinary power, which he certainly possessed, of getting under the skin of others and viewing the world through their eyes, and he compared this gift to djinns in the Arabian Nights who were able to assume human forms and direct their actions. Yet however strong this magic, however perceptive a man's observation, however intense his imagination, in the end he cannot cross the frontiers of his mind and character, and the world of Balzac or of Henry James is unmistakably their own, visible as their signatures, which display their own temperaments.

So the man dominates the work, and to the Napoleonic figure must be added that of the writer who created a world at least as distinctive as the world of Henry James (whose elegance never concealed his own Napoleonic quality). The essential difference of Balzac, more evident than a seam of vulgarity in him, no more important than the flaw of gentility in Henry James, was that there always remained in him something of a child, fascinated and excited by the disgraceful behaviour of grown-ups, whose misadventures he gleefully records, while Henry James appears elderly even in his earliest works. *La Comédie humaine* is above all an immense fairy story, stuffed with all those horrors at which only children have the fortitude not to shrink.

It is true that Balzac's astonishing powers of observation and his exact detail give to this fairy tale the accuracy and the proportions of a history, but its origin and its vitality were in his own childish fantasy. Henry James never showed himself a more faithful disciple of Balzac than when he claimed for the novelist the status of a historian, and his own novels are also documents. But Balzac was more insistent: he was even more exact than a historian, for he was—so he claimed—a secretary, and French society itself was the historian. He pointed out in his ·Preface to *La Comédie humaine* that neither Athens nor Rome had created a history of manners, for which posterity would willingly sacrifice some of their political records. To ensure that western civilisation would be better remembered, he recorded a history of manners in his age, a work that has since been called "a veritable encyclopaedia."

Yet even secretaries have private lives, compilers of encyclopaedias their passions. Balzac himself not only recognised this, but proclaimed that passion was the stuff of life, without which religion and history and art would have no purpose. So all the descriptions of the furniture in the houses of over two thousand women and men in his books, all the details of their coats, vests, dresses, and shoes, came second in his estimate to the chief passion of their lives. It is true that he set out to describe French society, but that was only the background to an exact expression of life itself.

The impossibility, the simplicity, and the absurdity of such an ambition could have issued only from the mind of a man with the confidence of a child. "When I grow up, I'll never go to bed." So children talk—and Balzac at times achieved that too, as he worked through nights kept awake by the black coffee which in the end was too much for his heart. Most children grow out of such ambitions, while Balzac not only held to his, not only expressed life, but created it, as no criminal is more living than Vautrin, no father more vivid than Goriot. Marcel Bouteron has declared that the reality of daily acquaintances is less than Balzac's figures, and Oscar Wilde maintained:

A steady course of Balzac reduces our living friends to shadows, and our acquaintances to the shadows of shades. His characters have a kind of fervent fiery-coloured existence. They dominate us, and defy scepticism.

Some children invent friends to whom they assign names and incidents more highly coloured than their own. Balzac retained this power, and it is a further proof of the child in him that he decided to become a great man before he decided to become a writer. That too is a common ambition with children: genius is only the realisation of that desire.

The portrait of Balzac at twenty by Achille Devéria shows the great candour of extreme youth. The Byronic pose only emphasizes that the features are still those of a child. Long years of toil and experience altered those features, as is evident in the Napoleonic pose of a likeness four years before his death, but, remarkably, death itself restored the earlier image, for the Giraud deathbed sketch shows a round and simple face almost more like a child than the man of twenty.

This was the last and most convincing evidence of the child Balzac surviving to the end. It is the most important element in his character, because it determined that of *La Comédie humaine,* which he once described as a western Arabian Nights. Even the cynicism and sophistication in it has the youthful abandon of a beginner with his first insight into what really goes on behind the scenes, and it is noticeable that the most cynical remarks are put into the mouths of young dandies, among whom Balzac at one time hoped to be numbered.

Childish exuberance is of course even more visible in those *œuvres de jeunesse,* not often published and less often read, which he wrote before he had made his name, not even giving his own name to them, but signing them with names of which the most aristocratic was Horace de Saint-Aubin, the most fantastic Lord R'hoone—an

anagram of his own Honoré. Some think this hackwork
has been too much neglected, for there are touches of
weird and comic invention in them, and it is certain that
they taught him technique, but they are childish in the
most obvious sense. Clearly Balzac was aware of this,
or he would not have preserved his own name for the
great work to come. But the interest here is that he
hoped by intense documentation and detail to impose
reality on the play of his imagination—and succeeded
so well that he has often been regarded as a realist. In
the first work that he signed with his own name—*Le
Dernier Chouan,* later *Les Chouans,* he studied the
ground at Fougères, questioned witnesses in the neighbourhood, documented himself fully. Yet *Les Chouans*
remains one of the most romantic of his novels.

What constitutes a romantic writer, and the romantic
movement itself is a dispute unnecessary here, for clearly
what was most romantic in Balzac was less the influence
of Walter Scott (greatly though he admired him) than
simply his own youth. If all countries have their romantic
period, of which they are afterwards a little ashamed
yet glad that they happened, this is even more true of
men themselves. Balzac's difference was that, for all his
wisdom, for all his disillusionment even, he never wholly
grew out of his romantic period, and in the last years of
his life was still grasping eagerly at the illusions of a
young man, even realising them in his marriage to a
Polish countess, whom he had pursued for eighteen
years, when destiny added the appropriate romantic
touch by fixing his death in the same year.

If his life is remarkably like one of his own novels,
this only gives more emphasis to the romantic impulse
which was behind both.

To be young and romantic is common enough, though
with most people the phase is brief, as they hasten to
dismiss their illusions or to substitute those of the society

in which they live, to prove themselves adult or sophisticated. What is astonishing in Balzac and in the
characters he created is that they persist in their illusions
with the obstinacy of children. They are often terrible
children, committing crimes, engaging in the most tor-
tuous of intrigues or financial deals, carried by their
passions into the arms of a woman, death, success, or
despair, but they are single-minded—as their creator who
worked in anguish through the nights when his lovers
and his criminals were also too occupied to sleep.

This obsessed quality has aroused the chief criticism
against Balzac, that his people are not human beings but
types, a Goriot who is more a father than a man, a
Grandet who is more a miser than a father, a duchesse
de Langeais who is more a duchess than a woman. Yet
they are true to their inner natures. They are Walter
Mittys who realise their fantasies, as Balzac realised his
childish resolve to be a great man. They have his own
intensity of will. As Baudelaire remarked, even his
dishwashers have genius.

So this sociological, scientific work, this description of
French society by a man who termed himself its secretary, turns out to be Balzac's personal world—for all
the density of its detail, for all the exact notes on people's
incomes and taxes, for all the patterns in their carpets and
the colour of their eyes. This is often levelled as a re-
proach against Balzac, but in essence it is a limitation
which personality itself imposes on all artists, recognised
in speaking of men or situations as Shakespearean. If this
charge is more often pressed against Balzac, it is largely
because he deliberately set limits to his own world by
bringing the same characters, whether politicians, duchesses, lawyers, or courtesans, into different novels. This
device of recurring characters served to enclose his society, almost into a separate state, a principality, as
M. Félicien Marceau has said, in which people are all not

only acquaintances, but interconnected and related, often accomplices.

Yet these characters are the most sharply differentiated, and they are mostly minor characters. The obsessed characters, apart from Vautrin, who has his own cycle of stories, are not recurrent: Claes, Grandet, Goriot live and die in their own novels. But it is precisely these who have most of Balzac's passion and genius in their blood. They resemble him, but they fulfil their lives in very different circumstances.

This contrast between the major and the minor figures represents a contrast in Balzac's own person between his original romantic impulse and the effort to impose exact detail and observed reality on the children of his imagination—an effort so powerful that some critics continue to accept him as essentially a historian of manners.

As a result, the chief division in Balzac criticism is between those who approach him from the severely documentary and those who view him from the more personal and romantic angle. The most forceful champion of his realism and documentation is Professor György Lukács, the Hungarian critic, who quotes Engels on Balzac's novels:

> . . . even about economic details I have learnt more from them than from all the books of all the professional historians, economists, and statisticians of the time. . . .

He further quotes Marx on Balzac's "deep understanding of real conditions." Even more remarkably, Professor Lukács, a Marxist himself, considers Balzac a far deeper realist than Zola, who only has "the outer trappings" of realism. Balzac is for this critic basically antiromantic.

On the other hand, M. Albert Béguin has developed a contrast in Balzac studies with his *Balzac visionnaire*, taking up Baudelaire's remark that he was surprised on the emphasis given to Balzac's observation, when he was above all a visionary, a passionate visionary. For M. Béguin, Balzac and his characters are "seeking the absolute and thirsting for eternity." When Balzac speaks in *Facino Cane*, as quoted above, of his gift for entering into the skins of others, M. Béguin sees this as "second sight" beyond ordinary human powers. For him Balzac has the gifts of a poet, and his desire to "tear words from silence and ideas from the night" recalls the intensity of Rimbaud.

One interesting point in these two opposed critics is that Professor Lukács gives special attention to *Les Paysans*, a work often neglected, finding in this the most acute analysis of nineteenth century capitalism, while M. Béguin thinks that Balzac's one weakness was his treatment of peasants, as he found them dull for a novelist because they were static, and he was concerned only with situations that were dynamic.

These opposed views have their own distinction and authority: Professor Lukács is widely respected as the most courageous and perceptive of Marxist critics, while M. Béguin has done distinguished work on modern French writers, edited an edition of Balzac, and dedicated his propositions on him to Marcel Bouteron, the dean of all Balzac analysts. Both critics too, though their views are so opposed, are ardent supporters of Balzac—authentic Balzacians.

It is easy, of course, to gloss over the difference by saying that Balzac is both a great realist observer and an intense visionary, and there is a truth in this compromise. But there are other divergences of opinion on Balzac which recall not only those of his own Napoleon, but the extraordinary theses advanced on Shakespeare, who has been identified with lawyers, statesmen, nobles, other dramatists, or assigned contradictory positions in religion

and politics. At least this places Balzac in the rank of
those comprehensive writers who are large enough to
figure as masters in any school.

Though he has sometimes been compared to Shakespeare, beyond the obvious analogy between *Goriot* and
Lear, only M. André Maurois has dared to say that of
the three monuments erected to humanity by Shakespeare, Balzac, and Tolstoy, *La Comédie humaine* is the
most comprehensive. It may be the greatest survey of
society, but the Spanish critic Eugenio d'Ors made a
useful distinction when he said that while Balzac is
enormous, Shakespeare is great, for this draws attention
to the monstrous element in Balzac which is too disproportionate for perfection. The vision and the poetry and
the delicacy of *A Midsummer-Night's Dream* belong to
a paradise not visible even in *Séraphita*, though Bottom
might have found a home in the *Contes drolatiques*. But
it is really only in his mastery of climax, as at the end of
Le Père Goriot or *La Cousine Bette*, that Balzac ap-
proaches Shakespeare.

Yet the distinction between them appears greater than
it is for reasons quite unconnected with their work.
Shakespeare, as Arnold said: "Didst tread on earth
unguess'd at.—Better so!"

The great blessing of Shakespeare is that he has no
biography. Nobody (despite the scholarly or absurd
efforts made) has been able to pull his work to pieces,
analyse the influence of this or that love, point to fixa-
tions, complexes, or compensations. His work remains
hermetically sealed, as if it had been presented on
graven tablets from a sacred mountain.

It is far otherwise with Balzac, alas. His documentation is immense—biographies, criticism, analyses, authentic facts, portraits, drawings, caricatures, descriptions of
his hands and his hats, his canes and his coffeepots

abound, while the women of his choice have been as
jealously preserved as the harem of a sultan.

The accidents of his life have been a further misfortune to him after death. As Lamartine realised at the
time, he was a great man to whom the fates had measured
a destiny hard to reconcile with greatness. It is not
only that everything to which he set his hand, only
excepting those achieved with the pen, turned out a failure or a fiasco, not only that his publishing house and
even the house he had built for him at Les Jardies
collapsed, that the paper he edited also sank under him,
that he was constantly vexed by debt and chased by
creditors, that the woman he loved longest kept him
waiting longest, it was not only that these and other
misfortunes cramped him, but that his sufferings belong
more to the world of his droll stories than to *La Comédie
humaine*. Not for him the solitary stoicism of a Vigny,
the beard or the exile of Hugo, the Cabinet rank of Lamartine. The greatest of the romantics, he suffered humilia-
tions that were too childish to achieve their touch of the
sublime—his own favourite adjective. Yet he suffered
more, and though he had the most powerful physique,
died younger than any of them, sacrificed to his work.

It may be that Shakespeare was ridiculed, endured
whips and scorns, the insolence of office, the pangs of
dispriz'd love; it may be that people laughed at his
yellow stockings or tricked him to hide in a laundry
basket, but at least no record remains beyond those
details which he transformed into the plays of his
imagination. He remains the author of his work.

Certainly Balzac remains the author of *La Comédie
humaine*, but he is also the centre of incidents and
escapades which were recorded not by himself, but by
malicious or envious colleagues, scandalmongers, and
enemies—or friends who were sometimes equally aston-

ished by his behaviour, though they judged it differently. It was the child in him that provoked most amusement, and the stories circulated about him in Paris were not unlike some told by parents of their own children, but they had a different effect when ascribed to a writer of genius.

It may be that his work would have been differently judged if less had been known of his life. Certainly he has been most honoured where he has been better known by his work. In 1835 he was applauded in Vienna when he was still the butt of Paris wits, and even over a dozen years later a spokesman of the French Academy announced that "We have no chair large enough for M. de Balzac." French critics were too sophisticated to understand the child in him. In Victorian England critics were too severe to welcome a writer who described with childish exuberance the escapades of duchesses and prostitutes, corrupt politicians and criminals. Something of this severity, moved to a literary plane, has survived in English critics. Mr. Geoffrey Brereton speaks distastefully of Balzac's presence in his books, "breathing heavily behind," while even Mr. Martin Turnell, who appreciates his enormities and accepts the point made by Baudelaire (on whom he has himself written with such penetration) that Balzac was more a visionary than an observer, will hardly allow him the place claimed by Balzacians.

It is in America, with the great Balzac bibliography created by Mr. W. H. Royce, in Germany and Austria, with the tributes of Stefan Zweig, that Balzac has been best appreciated. New York has its active Balzac Society, while South America has its Universal Balzac Society.

There is a reason for this: some degree of detachment is necessary to see the true position of Balzac in world literature, as the height of some peaks is better judged at a distance than when they are levelled or reduced by hills close around them. Local French and European prejudices have similarly intervened against Balzac. Critics belonging to the revolutionary tradition in France and liberals in England have resented his championship of the Church and monarchy, though Veuillot complained that "M. de Balzac supported the Church and the monarchy in such a manner that their enemies could applaud him." So to Swedenborgians he seemed too much of a Catholic, to Catholics too much of a Swedenborgian. Even in literature, outside politics or religion, other prejudices operated: for realists he was too romantic, for romantics too realistic.

Yet it is remarkable how many of his most fervent admirers have been writers who were themselves novelists, nor is this only because his position in the history of the novel is as unique as that of Raphael in the history of painting, so that an attempt to be pre-Balzacian might mark a theory no less than the term pre-Raphaelite. Of course it is possible to dislike either of these masters, to regret their influence, even to regard it as disastrous, and both painters and novelists have moved in directions quite opposed to their examples, yet they remain as points of reference, and anybody who practices their art feels an attraction or a repulsion for them. A contemporary French novelist, M. Félicien Marceau, expressed this when he said: "We are all children of *Le Père Goriot.*"

Goethe in the last year of his life recorded his admiration for *La Peau de chagrin*, which he used to show the inferiority of Hugo's *Notre-Dame de Paris*. Balzac has been criticized for simplicity in his analysis, yet novelists as subtle as Henry James and Proust have been devoted to him. More recently Mr. Somerset Maugham has declared that he is the only novelist to give him an impression of genius.

This consensus embodies a recognition by novelists that Balzac has the gift they most value, what is sometimes called "power," the ability to create an irrefutable impression of life. Maurice Baring, himself a novelist, described the gift in these terms:

> Balzac has a kind of obsessive power. He holds you with his glittering eye, like the Ancient Mariner; and once you take a plunge into a book of his you are obsessed by it as a dream, in spite of its great reality of detail.

This is the answer to the question posed by Professor Lukács and M. Béguin as to whether he is to be regarded as a realist or a visionary. The exact detail draws its reality only from the obsessive force of the dream, without which it would be as lifeless as Professor Lukács himself finds it in Zola. The power of his vision is the essence of Balzac.

It is natural enough to set this quality first, for if art were no more than the reproduction of reality, there would be no answer to the Jansenist gibe of Pascal, that painting is a vain attempt to arouse admiration for what is not admired in nature. Art is precisely that more intense vision which freshens nature, as the mind is refreshed in sleep. Balzac's intensity owed something to those long hours of work at night in which he discharged on paper the obsessions of his dreams.

This justifies Rodin's figure, whose head is so evidently that of Balzac the visionary, whose robe resembles a dressing gown worn in the nights of his labour. Yet it is the domination of this powerful figure which some critics resent, finding it hard to reconcile either with the child in Balzac or with the very human escapades and misfortunes of his life. So it remains a question of figures —the many images of Balzac presented in portraits and in caricatures, presented or misrepresented—a question of which is to be accepted.

Certainly it is impossible to dissociate him wholly from his life, as a Shakespeare has been so happily liberated from his. Yet critics admit that who he was cannot increase or lessen the greatness of Shakespeare's plays. So the follies or disillusions of Balzac's life cannot affect the proportions of *La Comédie humaine*. To argue otherwise would be no less absurd than to maintain that because, as Vasari records, Michelangelo wore his leather leggings for months, and tore the skin when he at last discarded them, his statues must have feet of clay. The follies of great men have their interest, but it is an interest which is inspired only by their work.

If, when all these reservations have been made, the figure of Balzac continues to intrude, it is surely because he was a great man in his own right. He had the energy, the intellectual capacity, above all the strength of will to achieve greatness, and it was an accident of destiny that he attained this in literature. Lytton Strachey, an adverse critic of his style, admits that his genius is irresistible. Sometimes this genius appears almost naked—like Rodin's other statue of Balzac—and shocks by its appearance in a small masterpiece where it seems out of place.

For this reason his reputation has always stood higher with his fellow writers and with his readers than with critics. He fascinates no less by the personality in his work than by the work itself. Contact with this personality is an acquired taste which creates Balzacians, addicts more comparable to a sect or to collectors than to the ordinary run of readers. Here again is a parallel with Henry James, for he too is an acquired taste, but while he transformed himself into a style, Balzac transformed himself into characters, every one of whom has something of his excessive will to live.

In this crowd of figures, two stand out as peculiarly images of Balzac himself, Vautrin the man of disguises, the rebel against society, who knows all its secrets, who finishes on the side of the police, Vautrin the criminal who is also Herrera the priest, and Goriot, the father who lives only in his daughters. For these are the two leading passions of Balzac, to penetrate everywhere and to project himself in his children, whom he had created. The fervour of this last passion is proved by the fact that while he spoke often enough of his sufferings and his disappointments, his creative verve was not interrupted, nor his exuberance checked, and one of the rare occasions when he admitted depression and an inability to work was after receiving the news that the child born to him by Madame Hanska had died. Something of this tragedy passed into *La Cousine Bette* on which he was then engaged.

Always the most important part of his life passed into his work, and he figures so largely in this that Balzac studies owe more to Swiss, American, French, and German scholars who have concentrated on different aspects of *La Comédie humaine* than to critics in France and in England who have judged him on their own literary principles, on which he may not be the greatest of novelists. For *La Comédie humaine* is not simply a collection of novels, but the attempt of one man to lead many different lives at every level of society. It is a vision of the extraordinary possibilities of life.

There has been increasing recognition of this presence of Balzac in his work, particularly by M. Gaëtan Picon who speaks of him creating his own life in his work, and by Dr. Herbert J. Hunt, whose recent *Balzac's Comédie Humaine* is the finest treatment in English of the work as a whole. Dr. Hunt has chosen to analyse *La Comédie humaine*, not in the final divisions assigned to it, but in the order in which the various novels and stories were written, which produces very interesting results, as he shows that Balzac's main preoccupations at the time he was writing found expression in his work.

The question of images can be answered only in relation to that work, for the choice is not between the

Napoleonic image of Rodin and the caricatures of Paris papers, nor even between the romantic and the realist, but between the two-thousand-odd characters of *La Comédie humaine*. If Goriot seems the closest, that is because Balzac was the father, the creator of that monstrous progeny.

An Entry into Life

O<small>N THE</small> 29th of May, 1799, the feast of St. Mary Magdalene, patron of many women in his work, Honoré was born at Tours to a mother aged twenty-one and a father of fifty-three (whose name had originally been Balssa) charged with commissioning supplies for the 22d Division of the revolutionary army.

Born in the last year of the eighteenth century, Honoré de Balzac, as he later called himself, died at the age of fifty-one just in the middle of the nineteenth century, and these limits—with a few exceptions, most in the philosophical section—were roughly those of *La Comédie humaine*.

Touraine had already given to France Rabelais, Ronsard, and Descartes. Of these Rabelais was much the most important to Balzac—he described his *Peau de chagrin* as an offering before the statue of Rabelais, "whose immortal satire has already seized the future and the past of mankind in its grip." Rabelais showed his presence even more clearly in the *Contes drolatiques,* where Balzac invoked this "eternal glory of Touraine," and said he wrote to show himself "a good son of Touraine and to regale the hearty appetite of the great people in this sweet land of plenty." In *L'Illustre Gaudissart* he added:

The love of wit and banter, clever tricks and good stories, which marks every page of Rabelais's work, accurately reflects the spirit of Touraine that has the refinement of manners proper to a country where the Kings of France long held their court.

It was only in Touraine that Gaudissart, who could outwit Parisians, was himself outwitted. Yet the exuberant element in Balzac's character probably owed more to the Gascon blood that he inherited from his father (whose family came from the region of the Pyrenees) than to Touraine, for his was essentially a meridional temperament, and his sympathies went further south, into Spain and Italy, whose passionate nature he often praised in contrast with coldness and calculation in the people of Paris and northern France.

He owed less to his mother, for she can be credited, apart from bringing him into the world, only with his unhappy childhood, largely owing to her, which stimulated his self-reliance and strength of will, as he soon learned that he was an exception, and that he had to depend on his own efforts. He even maintained that he had never really had a mother, and this was true in that he was put out to a nurse until the age of four—a custom at that time less peculiar than his again being boarded out until the age of seven, then sent to a school from which he never returned home for the holidays. But it was less this upbringing than the lack of affection in his mother which rankled. Two years before his death he wrote to her that he had no desire for her to pretend to an affection which she had never felt, as all this had been given to his brother Henri (who was almost certainly not the son of her husband). He even added that she had been a "good mother" for him, in the sense that he had escaped being spoiled as Henri was. This was his ironical gratitude to her for his unhappy childhood.

Her treatment of Honoré, her first child, argues a
certain resentment of her husband which her fondness
for Henri, not his child, confirms. This husband was
coarser than herself, not only in the ordinary masculine
sense, but in his indifference to her social superiority.
He was also old enough to be her father, and her distaste
for him had the aristocratic disdain of Anastasie and
Delphine for their father Goriot, who was also a commissioner of supplies to the army.

Even apart from circumstances, this wife and mother
was a difficult woman, hard and insensitive, one model
for *La Cousine Bette* in her bitterness. At one time
her children feared that she might be out of her mind, but
the doctor kindly reassured them, "No, she is not mad,
only malicious." She was a woman much given to re-
proaching, the worst sort to live with.

Yet when her son began to earn money, and even
before he became a well-known writer, she was affected
by his ambition, his energy, his strength of will, enough
to lend him money, and as he lost or spent it and earned
more she became involved in his speculations, which
gave her both the hope of gain and the chance of more
bitter reproaches. There remained some tie between
them, more material than moral, yet something more than
the cash nexus, for there was in it the sort of bitter
relationship found in other Latin households, nourished
to greater strength more by resentment than by affection.
After she became a widow—the father died in the year
that the son first signed his name to a book—her financial
and reproachful interests in her son's affairs kept her
grasping and active. She even survived him, a more
natural figure by his deathbed than by his cradle—not a
lovable character, but a very Balzacian one, the first
of those horrible visions which fascinate because they are
pockmarked with truth.

Her neglect of him was the chief element in his childhood, for it provoked that passionate desire for love and fame which prompted both his most disastrous and most triumphant actions. He wanted the love he had never received as a child, and he wanted to show his mother and family that others could acclaim what they had not valued. Even at school he was considered dull, because he read and reflected deeply on subjects outside the term's work. This constant refusal of recognition forced him, like some of his characters, to a point where the only alternatives were suicide or a fantastic self-confidence issuing in triumph.

The transformation of the dull boy into the genius becomes less obscure owing to his own account of his schooldays in *Louis Lambert*. This is often regarded as a poor novel, but even apart from its interest for this development, it remains the most absorbing document on the awakening of intellectual curiosity. Others have written in many languages of the first movements of love in youth, but this intellectual adolescence which can be even more intoxicating has rarely been treated, for the awakening of the mind is much harder to express than that of the emotions or the body, as in many lives it never happens at all, and there is no common experience for reference.

Yet Balzac contrives in some of these pages to express his own wonder at a first entry into the world of ideas, as if it were an entry into some more enchanted palace of the Arabian Nights. In the person of Louis he tells of the excitement with which he read even a dictionary, as words and ideas were scattered on the ground of a mind where they flowered into fantastic shapes—for this boy neglected by his family and despised by his masters was an infant prodigy. He had a child's curiosity and wonder, asking senseless questions which nevertheless required an intellectual answer. Why is the colour green so predominant in nature? Why is the straight line an invention of man, hardly to be found in the structure of the world, where organic life is expressed in curves?

He read with the indiscriminate enthusiasm of all young and enquiring minds, but he retained an astonishing mass of detail which prompted more questions. Why should Bacon become ill at an eclipse of the moon, Tycho Brahe at the sight of a fox, Erasmus at the smell of fish, Bayle at the sound of water? Such odd items fascinated Balzac, because it was from the antipathies and sympathies between men and their environment that he achieved the vision of a novelist, which developed from the vision of this schoolboy philosopher, who found it so difficult to distinguish between mind and matter. A certain disposition of features, he argued, or a peculiarity in the organic structure of the brain was sufficient to produce a Raphael, a Napoleon, or a Beethoven, while a valley deprived of sunshine could account for mental defects no less remarkable. How then was it possible to distinguish between material and mental causes? The only answer, he concluded, was that thought itself was a material substance.

This conclusion, that might lead to the materialism of which Balzac was later accused, had just the opposite effect on his Louis, who went on to identify light, the principle of life, with religion—St. John's "light that lightens every man coming into the world." He thought that there had never been more than one religion, that of the mystics—a belief similar to that of another brilliant child, Aldous Huxley. Louis declared:

> Zoroaster, Moses, Buddha, Confucius, Jesus Christ, Swedenborg had the same principles, devoted themselves to the same end. But the last of all, Swedenborg, will perhaps be the Buddha of the North.

All this, though offered only as the eager imaginings of the child Louis, had some place in the mind of the later Balzac, when he had not much trouble in reconciling it with his propaganda for the Church, for it was the age of Catholic romantics—Novalis and the Brentanos in Germany, Chateaubriand in France, Manzoni in Italy. The Church had then a romantic appeal, and devotion was better appreciated than doctrine.

Louis, like Balzac himself, was really more interested in supernatural phenomena and the occult than in religion, for they were the justification of his theory that thought and will were material forces, which revealed themselves in second sight, levitation, sorcery, visions, and miracles. He always referred to the "occult sciences," respectable to his view as any other, and in fact he respected them more.

Judgement on such matters has no place in the study of a novelist, and some have lightly dismissed them. M. Marceau, in his perceptive study of Balzac's world, expressly omits *Séraphita,* the most Swedenborgian work, with the plea that it is outside his province. But this obsession with the occult and the interpenetration of mind and matter are very important to an understanding of Balzac, because they explain both his extraordinary emphasis on material detail and the oddly obsessive quality which this assumes. The more material the scene, the more intense is the gaze of the visionary Balzac. It is not surprising that there has been such confusion among critics in deciding whether he is a realist or a visionary, because, as he discloses in *Louis Lambert,* that confusion was his philosophy of life.

Philosophers may smile or frown at this, but there can be little doubt that it greatly increased his power as a novelist, for a novelist can create the illusion of life only by pressing the minds of his characters and their material surroundings together to make a convincing unity. Philosophers may be able to confine themselves to ideas, but novelists have constantly to be shaping theirs into figures and furniture, incomes, smiles, or dresses, as women and men often express themselves less in words than in a turn of the head, a style of hat, or the choice of a chair. Balzac's belief in the occult and in the strange power which makes some the slaves of their surroundings and enables others to transform them, however questionable in itself, impelled him to write fairy stories which are yet wholly real. Sometimes, as in *La Peau de chagrin*, or such stories as *L'Elixir de longue vie*, or *Melmoth réconcilié*, he deliberately introduced the supernatural, but their atmosphere is hardly different from others apparently realistic, as his mind was so charged with visions that reality became for him a manifestation of the occult.

Louis Lambert is one of his least successful stories, for it is more an exposition of these ideas than an application of them, less a novel than a treatise, like that Treatise on the Will to which Louis had given the whole genius of his youth only to have it torn from him by a master and destroyed. He was constantly being caned for lack of attention, but when he looked up there was something in his gaze that led the master to say, "Look at me again like that, Lambert, and you'll be caned." So schooldays passed between abstraction and the cane. Nor was Balzac's life very different afterwards, for when he looked up from his work, it was usually only to receive some blow from fate.

At the end of these six years in the Collège de Vendôme he returned to his family at Tours, but shortly afterwards they moved to Paris, where after more schooling he was sent out into an office to study law under Maître Merville, a man who had the rare distinction to Balzac of being honest in his practice—as he was the model for Derville, to whom le Colonel Chabert went for legal confirmation of his identity. Balzac showed further regard for this honest man of law by dedicating to him

Un Épisode sous la Terreur, "to explain to those who want to know everything where I learned enough of legal procedure to conduct the affairs of my little world."

He learned enough for that, and he learned much from the false starts of these years, as there were still more before him even when he abandoned law, and at the age of twenty proclaimed to his family that he was going to be a writer. Matters were not helped when he read aloud his tragedy *Cromwell* to the family and a professor was summoned to give judgement, which was that his time could be better employed than at writing tragedies.

It was a bad year for the family, one in which the father's brother had been guillotined for murder. The mother had great opportunity for reproaches—but Balzac, strong in his theory of the will, stood firm. Finally it was agreed that he should be given an allowance of fifteen hundred francs, some two hundred dollars, to live for a year or two while he established his reputation as a writer. He managed to write and even to publish books, but they were so short of his dreams that he refused to sign them, and it was nearly ten years before he made his name.

The years from 1819 to 1829, from twenty to thirty in his own life, were his real schooling, for he had hardly been able to educate himself at school, interrupted as he was by canes and masters and lessons. In the garret in which his meagre allowance enabled him to live, close to the Place de la Bastille, he was at last free to read and write. He must have read prodigiously, for *La Comédie humaine* is stuffed with information, theories, facts, and later he had no time to read—nor to observe. When asked where he observed his characters, he retorted indignantly, "Observe? How do you think I have time to observe, when I have barely time to write?"

That is one more sign that he was a writer of vision, not a reporter of fact, but all the same the range of knowledge in his work shows wide reading, and the background of detail shows much observation. Marx himself was something of a visionary, but he was also an economist, and if both he and Engels regarded Balzac as a chief authority on social and economic subjects, it is evident that studies, not only of books, but of people and places in Paris, went to achieve this mastery.

When Balzac said that he had no time except for writing, that was in his great productive period between the ages of thirty and fifty. He knew then that this expenditure of energy, in disregard of health and sleep, would shorten his life, as this was the moral of *La Peau de chagrin,* almost the first work of the period, and already time had for him the shorter perspective that comes to a man who foresees the year of his death. But the perspective was very different in the ten years between twenty and thirty, when he still enjoyed the immortality of youth. Time itself had a different quality then. He failed at everything he attempted, he was abjectly poor, and he was harassed by debt—but he could afford time. He used it largely and without discipline, reading and observing without discrimination. The discipline came later, when he sorted the accumulated material into *La Comédie humaine.*

He described these years, shortening them to intensify the crisis, at the beginning of *Un Drame au bord de la Mer:*

> This age, which for all men comes between twenty-two and twenty-eight, is the time of great thoughts and first conceptions, because it is the age of vast desires, the age when one has no doubts: to doubt is to be impotent. After this age, swift as seed-time, comes that of achievement.

Those years were also the ones in which he was most under the influence of Madame de Berny—another reason why he fixed the limits just there, for Pauline is with him there in Brittany (the setting of the story), and the name Pauline here, as in *Louis Lambert* or *La Peau de chagrin,* is usually a sign of Madame de Berny in his mind.

The influence of Madame de Berny can hardly be exaggerated, nor was Balzac exaggerating when he wrote at her death to Madame Hanska that she had been to him more than a friend, more than a mother, "more than any person can be to another." He had no need to say that to the woman who was eventually to become his wife, no need beyond the pressure of truth.

His original gifts, the strength of his will, the reading, the observation, the experience of these ten years between twenty and thirty, all were summed up in the person of Laure de Berny, for without her the whole personality of Balzac would have been different—if he had survived, for he was often driven to the limit of endurance, and it was she alone who sustained him with consolation and with joy.

It is often said that Balzac's women are more vivid, more finely conceived, and better characters than his men. His first great publishing success, *Physiologie du mariage,* was a defense of women and a demand for their emancipation, while women were the most passionate readers of his stories, especially those, such as *La Femme de trente ans,* which insisted that older women were the more attractive (fashion and relative ages have so changed that his "women of thirty" had then more the implications of a woman of forty or even fifty today). To express all this, he found a phrase, "It is only the last love of a woman which can satisfy the first love of a man," which contains a truth beyond the question of relative ages, as it discloses that women are always the experts, men always the beginners in this matter. All

this he learned from Madame de Berny, and all his
tributes to women as well as most of his knowledge of
them came originally from her.

She tried to eradicate his worst faults, and what
remain of them for some critics of his work—an awk-
wardness, exaggeration, or grossness, a childish straining
after effect, or bad manners, or social lapses—were
precisely the ones which she exerted herself to overcome.

On the other hand, some of his lesser faults, which have
a charm to a confirmed reader of Balzac, as eccentricities
in an old friend, his passion for great ladies, his devotion
to obsolete royalist ideas, his snobbery, or his purple
passages about women, these too echo his loyalty to
Madame de Berny, who was a godchild of Louis XVI
and Marie Antoinette, for whom the Duc de Richelieu
and the Princesse de Chimay had acted at her baptism.

She may be said to have formed Balzac in these de-
cisive years of his youth, for apart from his reading, it was
to her that he owed most of his education, in the sense
that this is a judgement on the real experience of life—
the most valuable education of a novelist.

The de Bernys had lived close to the Balzacs in Paris,
and when both families had moved out to Villeparisis a
chance arose for Balzac to become tutor to the de Bernys'
son Alexandre. He had already begun on his literary
hackwork, earning money where he could. Madame de
Berny had no fondness for the Balzacs, but she was
astonished by the gifts of their son, shocked by their
waste on worthless scribblings. She could see too that he
lacked any sympathy or direction. He was delightfully
naïve, brilliant, and horribly awkward. At home he had
that terrible woman, his mother, and a father who
shrugged and let her go her own way, as crude as he was
indifferent.

Madame de Berny was moved in more ways than one,
in her maternal indulgence, in her admiration for a

brilliant young man—who also had brilliant brown eyes—
in her pity for his loneliness and lack of success, in
the certainty that she could help and guide, perhaps even
inspire him.

It was a temptation to any woman, in that virtue itself
demanded that she should succour him. Any dangers in
the situation could be ridiculed by the certainty that
she was twenty-two years older than he was. But his good
humour was always proof against ridicule, and when
she teased him he only took it as the sort of teasing
natural to lovers.

Both had much to endure at home; both needed sympathy. Her husband was a man of black humours who
had only just escaped the guillotine, and he was perm-
anently embittered as if resentful at the loss of this exceptional privilege. In his own style he was as difficult a
character as Balzac's mother, who in her crises asked her
family for a heavy stone to take with her when she
threw herself into the Seine. Neither household was very
gay.

Madame de Berny had a generous and indulgent
nature. Her portrait reveals one of those women who
cannot help being indulgent—as Balzac, in Lamartine's
words, could not help being good-natured. It was not a
one-sided affair, for though she had much to give him,
she had suffered much, and he was as eager to console
her as she was to guide him.

She announced of course with a proper firmness that
she was going to be a mother to him, but it was already
a little late for that, as he had managed without a mother
for over twenty years, and in that time his masculine
assertion and his strength of will had developed, precisely because he had to rely on himself alone. It was more
important that his virile nature in the full ardour of youth
had been without a woman; and that was less easy to
manage. Laure de Berny appeared to him as the only

woman in his life, in understanding and in affection
certainly, but also in passion.

It is obvious enough that the absence of a mother's
affection was an important element in the matter and in
his whole life, but it is also true that he was often a
child in later life, and that his unique regard for Madame
de Berny was caused more by her qualities and the fondness of his gratitude than by the conventional substi-
tution of a "mother figure." Certainly he began by writing
to her that he was and would always be "excessively shy,
passionately loving, and so reserved that I dare not
confess my love." But that was itself not only a confession
but a declaration, and soon he was pointing out to her the
advantages of possessing a young lover, even saying how
useful he could be to her children.

This love of a younger man for an older woman had
been a Greek tradition, as readers of Mr. Thornton
Wilder's *Woman of Andros* will recall, and it had become
a French one, especially in the eighteenth and nineteenth
centuries, when women so dominated intellectual and
social life that admission to their salons was essential to
a young writer, who courted them both for their own
sake and his. Madame de Berny was not in that sense
a Madame Recamier or a Delphine Gay, still less a
George Sand, but she was able to guide and groom him
towards the salons of success.

She gave him all that she had to give, even money, for
dismayed by his hackwork, she allowed herself to
become involved in his schemes for making the money
which would give him leisure to write more honestly—
she urged that he was degrading himself in such cheap
historical romances as *Le Centenaire* or *Wann-Chlore*
(later changed to *Jane la pâle*). Posterity has generally
confirmed Madame de Berny's opinion that this was a
waste of Balzac, but it is less easy to judge whether the

cause was cynicism or incompetence, for he was only learning his technique at this stage, and these *œuvres de jeunesse* show traces of his real self, particularly on the Rabelaisian and the occult side, though his realism appears more rarely—touches in the beginning of *Argow le pirate*—and in one or two, *L'Israélite* and *La Dernière fée*, there is real cynicism in the endings—an obvious impatience to conclude the improbable story.

The later Balzac has been accused of cynicism on social issues, but never of this literary sort—and his endings are often his finest achievements. The early failure seems more a result of despair and a desire to be rid of the manuscript, perhaps with a resolve that the next would be better. Balzac himself confirmed Madame de Berny's opinion at the time by not signing these romances with his own name, and later by not including them in *La Comédie humaine.*

He at least wrote, acquired the habit of writing and telling a story, and when Urbain Canel, the publisher of *Jane la pâle*, spoke of publishing classics and requiring capital, Balzac, both for a respite from this sad business and the hope of profit, raised Balzac and de Berny money to become a publisher. He wrote an introduction to the works of Molière (a more lasting influence with him than Scott), and awaited a rush from the public, but the booksellers paid him with notes which he was unable to collect—a trick later adopted by some of his characters.

Bankruptcy encouraged him to start a printing business, for he argued that as publishers thrive on authors, so printers thrive on publishers: his active brain worked out such sequences logically but applied them too rapidly, as later when he went to Sardinia to exploit a silver mine neglected since Roman days, prophesied a success which actually followed—but to the profit of a fellow-traveller who left him to go to Genoa for the concession.

The printing business which he set up in the narrow rue Visconti, behind St. Germain des Prés, suffered from this same optimism and good nature. He was too quick and too sanguine, but his will and his enthusiasm must have been compelling, as they could even induce his mother to invest and to lose money—for these ventures left debts of a hundred thousand francs, perhaps less than twelve thousand dollars, which might not appear excessive when later set against the income of a famous and prolific writer, but he was constantly struggling to pay them and never succeeding because his costs of production, with innumerable corrections, were so extravagant—and even his economies became extravagances, as when he built himself a house to save the cost of an apartment. His optimism was as remarkable as his pessimism, but this was more natural than might appear, as the optimism sprang wholly from himself, while the pessimism came from his hard experience of the world.

The optimism survived, stronger than debts or disappointments, and was even fortified by the pessimism, because despite his desire for money and fame he refused to accept the values of the world. He juggled with money, gave exact accounts of income to his characters, calculated their rents, amassed piles of figures, gloated over coins with old Grandet, over bills of exchange with Gobseck, over vast manipulations of credit with Nucingen, but here he was only repeating the fantasies of his publishing and printing business. The essential point in his character was that he never took money seriously, not as it is taken seriously by real businessmen, real lawyers, or even by men living carefully on their incomes. For he never lived on his income, only on his hopes.

It is an important point, because his concern with money and the increasing part played by capital in society are often urged as proof of his realism, especially by Marxists, who have been quite hypnotized by his joyous juggling with figures. Yet he is remote from their materialism because his misers and capitalists are fantastic figures. He is not even denouncing them wholly, for he shares their childish enthusiasm for coins and rents, as he played with money in his own life. The final absurdity is reached when the dying Grandet, knowing that his great fortune has now to pass to his only child, Eugénie, urges her to take care, "For you will have to give an account of it to me one day." This proves, Balzac ironically adds, that Christianity should really be the religion of misers.

He is a realist in the sense that he saw money and love as two of the most powerful motives in human affairs, and he saw too that the disorderly pursuit of them often ended in disaster. But to see that, it is not necessary to be either a realist or a Marxist: it is only necessary not to be a fool.

Balzac was no fool. He was indeed a genius—of which one definition is an exaggerated love of the normal— and he had a genial trick of exaggerating these basic motives in human nature, precisely because anybody wholly under the influence of love or money himself exaggerates their importance. So when he writes of women and love, such phrases as "sublime creatures" or "ineffable delights" flow readily in his pages. In just the same style when he writes of money, francs, rents, mortgages, debts, profits, millions, they pile up hardly less sublimely, for he moves among these figures as among those others, the seductive shapes of his harem.

That his treatment of money has in it more of fantasy than finance is shown by his indulgence towards the tricks used to procure it, whether by the duchesse de Maufrigneuse or courtesans such as Esther or Carabine.

It is with relish that he relates such escapades, because he sympathized with those who took material values lightly. As Lamartine observed:

> His child-like serenity viewed the world from such a height that it seemed to him hardly more than a joke, a soap-bubble due to a child's fancy.

He was contemptuous of those writers and journalists who sold their gifts to the highest bidder, that prostitution of talent against which Madame de Berny had warned him. The grim pages of *Illusions perdues* reveal a disgust with such transactions, but they lighten when a Coralie cheats her protector for the benefit of her lover. He was no less indulgent towards thieves who only inconvenienced the rich, more than towards bankers and financiers who ruined hundreds of homes.

In fact, he can be more easily accused of irresponsibility towards money than of excessive regard for wealth. His own incursions into business had taught him that the innocent suffered and the guilty prospered in a society where speculation had advanced more rapidly than safeguards against fraud. He tried to pay his creditors, but he tried even harder to keep out of their hands, and at the end of his ten years' apprenticeship to the debts and despairs of Paris, he escaped to Brittany, where at Fougères he was welcomed by the Baron de Pommereul, a friend of the family.

The verve of the stories he related in the evening delighted his hosts. Madame de Pommereul said that his "perpetual good humour was so exuberant that it was contagious." After some of his tales, they asked, "Is it true?" At which he laughed and replied, "Not a word of truth in it—pure Balzac."

There was more truth in the work produced there, for which he solidly documented himself in the neighbourhood, but this book, *Le Dernier Chouan* (later *Les Chouans*) was also nearer to being pure Balzac. At least it was both the first signed with his name and the first to be worthy of it.

In *Les Chouans*—called after the owls whose cry identified the Breton royalists—the influence of Scott is still apparent, and even the subject is similar, as these Bretons were comparable to the Jacobites in their loyalty to a king over the border if not across the water. Balzac later declared in the Preface to *La Comédie humaine* that Scott had raised the novel to the philosophical level of history, but had not advanced from that to describe an entire society. In making this advance himself, he naturally began with the historical novel, which had first inspired him, gradually finding his way into the novel of contemporary manners in which he achieved mastery. In this he also freed himself from the more fantastic improbabilities so evident in the historical romances of his hackwork. As the novel became more contemporary, it became more probable, for even today readers tolerate greater violations of fact in a historical romance than in a novel set in the age they know. Yet the old habit died hard, and one or two improbabilities recur even in a work so skilful as *La Femme de trente ans* when the daughter elopes with a pirate (to recall the unsigned *Argow le pirate*), though her mother is a most subtle study of a woman married to an *homme nul*—Balzac's term for a man whom a woman can make nothing of. Such lapses justify Madame de Berny's warning against the waste of his gifts, and prove how much he—and his readers—owe to her.

Les Chouans, appropriately enough, describes events that happened in the year of his birth, 1799. So from this first novel he went on to describe society through the first half of the nineteenth century and the whole of his own life, and though the process followed no exact order, the last written were set in years closest to their own date.

Les Chouans is only the first in time, not in quality, though Balzac in this story already transforms the historical novel by the skill of his political intrigue. The love between the royalist leader and the woman who is a republican agent has been compared to that of Romeo and Juliet, for they too have only one night to share before their death. Yet this novel was hardly enough to make Balzac's name, which became known with *Physiologie du mariage,* published in the same year, 1829, as this created a scandal with its revolutionary demands for more freedom to girls before marriage and with the cynicism of its anecdotes, offered as a warning to husbands. Its originality was the real shock.

From this year 1829 until 1846 he was almost constantly productive, often publishing more than half a dozen works a year, of unequal length and value, but in some years, as in 1833 and 1835, issuing two or three major works in a single year. Of over ninety works, most appeared in these eighteen years, and at the end of this period he still had many more planned, but lacked the health and the strength to continue.

In 1830 he had already proved his mastery of the shorter novel and the short story, with the publication of *Scènes de la vie privée,* and in the following year he achieved his first great success with a full-length novel, *La Peau de chagrin,* which has a special importance both as an allegory of all human life, a *Pilgrim's Progress* which was also a *Rake's Progress,* and as a prophetic account of his own end—for even as early as 1834 he wrote: "It will be curious to see the author of *La Peau de chagrin* die young."

This is the book that most clearly expresses Balzac's philosophy of life: that every desire of a man is an expenditure of energy that weakens his vitality, and ends by killing him.

Simply stated, this is obviously true of those who kill themselves by debauchery or by overwork, but he applied it very much more widely to include every act of the will, which issues in the impulses or passions, the thoughts or feelings of men. Thought itself was no less destructive than passion, unless controlled and tamed by education, philosophy, or religion.

This was the essence of Balzac's belief, that men are killed by the strength of their own desires. So Goriot is killed by his passion for his daughters, Claes by his search for the Absolute, Hulot by his lust for women—and Balzac by his frenzy to finish *La Comédie humaine*.

The belief can be questioned as a general principle, on the grounds that these men were mad or unbalanced, that they were projections of Balzac's own frenzy. *La Peau de chagrin* answers this objection by viewing the process of desire in slow motion, to show that it applies also to ordinary men, whose lesser desires are just as destructive on a smaller scale. So they arrive more slowly at the same end. The principle remains the same.

To illustrate this principle, Balzac used—for the only time in a major work—a magic device, an old faded piece of leather, the skin of a wild ass, on which is engraved the seal of Solomon and a phrase in Sanskrit: the wishes of its owner will all be granted at the cost of his own life, for as each wish is fulfilled the skin will shrink, until nothing remains of either.

Raphael, on the verge of suicide, goes into a remarkable antique shop, the description of which is one of the great Balzac passages, evocative as that of Madame Vauquer's boardinghouse. Here an old man offers him the skin, and expounds the great principle—only knowledge can bring peace.

The old antiquary claims that he has found the only

true enjoyment of the world, because he has contemplated all its treasures and beauties without expending his desires on them. He has preserved his health and his strength because he has never wasted them in the search for pleasure. He has an "imaginary harem" in which he can enjoy women he has never seen. Why should anybody prefer to admire "flesh that is more or less colored, forms that are more or less rounded"?

Knowledge is the only wisdom, madness is the excess of desire. Raphael is unconvinced—he prefers to take the magic skin which will satisfy his desires, the first of which is an evening of luxury. At once he runs into an old friend who says he has been looking for him everywhere, as a rich banker is giving a party to launch a paper where Raphael's gifts will be rewarded. In the aftermath of this party, where wines and women are lavishly provided, he expresses a second wish for riches of his own, and falls into conversation with a lawyer who is looking for the heir to a millionaire Major O'Brien, dead in India. Raphael's mother was an O'Brien.

The art of *La Peau de chagrin* is that all the wishes are fulfilled naturally, so naturally that Raphael at first feels that the skin is not responsible, until at the granting of a wish he feels the skin contract in his hand. The results are also natural, for wealth affects him much as any other young man. The magic—as Goethe pointed out—in no way interferes with the natural course of life, and the background remains wholly realistic. But the contraction of the skin serves to point the moral, the destructive power of desire, and even this change in the skin has its counterpart in similar reactions of tissue to disease and death. The choice of a wild ass for the skin probably came from Rabelais's phrase about controlling the ass of the body.

Poor Raphael tried to control his skin by the aid of

science, but while biologists could define it, and chemists could subject it to treatment, they were powerless to enlarge it. So when his own condition deteriorated, three doctors argued over his symptoms, one insisting that the trouble was organic, another that it was psychological, a third that it was both. None could cure him, as none could extend the skin: they could only define its properties, or his case: "Science had given him all that it has to offer—a nomenclature."

Passionately interested in science though he was, Balzac here shows his own power of vision by seeing even then what has since become more apparent, that science is more apt to define and measure than to cure the ills of humanity. The arguments of his scientists and doctors have his own realism, but they issue in a satire which is again in the tradition of Rabelais.

Raphael's only course was to live as a recluse, in order to avoid any occasion of desire, and so preserve what remained of the skin. He is nearly saved by the devotion of Pauline—a Laure de Berny figure—and because she loves him already, his desire for her has no effect on the skin, which cannot grant a wish already fulfilled. But inevitably even she provokes him to further desires, and he dies in a final gust of passion which consumes his skin.

This was certainly the course of Balzac's life, as he often said that his only desires were for love and fame, and he destroyed himself in his frenzy for them. Even then he seems to have foreseen that, of all the women he loved, only the influence of Madame de Berny was wholly good. Zulma Carraud, his best friend and wisest adviser, never figured among them, though she once told him that she was the sort of woman he should have married. But he was never realist enough to find such a woman for himself, and with the great success of *La Peau de chagrin* he threw himself into the illusions of the world, dressed as a dandy, enjoyed the delights of fame. His own *Début dans la vie* was attended with the ridicules which he later ascribed to poor Oscar.

Yet he worked with the same frenzy: 1832 and 1833 saw the publication of the first *Contes drolatiques, Le Curé de Tours, Eugénie Grandet, Le Médecin de campagne,* the beginning of *Histoire des treize,* and many shorter pieces. In 1834 he began *Le Père Goriot,* and with its publication in the following year he was already in the centre of *La Comédie humaine.*

Le Père Goriot

ONE CONSEQUENCE of Balzac's fertility and the scope of his achievement is the difficulty of appreciating him by a single book. A Spanish critic has expressed this by saying that his work is not synoptic, that a general view is better obtained by a study of Balzac himself than by reading only one of his writings. His fame rests on *La Comédie humaine,* which in the most compact edition extends to ten volumes, each having more than a thousand closely printed pages. By arranging its parts in this order under a single title, he himself insisted on the unity of the whole.

It is a difference in architecture, of books no less than towns: some such as New York from the sea or Paris from the Sacré Cœur present a skyline not unworthy of the whole, others such as London or Milan offer no single point of focus. But it would be foolish to judge their importance or even their size from what is simply a difference of design. All have to be judged in their greatest monuments, and there are reasons for the general opinion that *Le Père Goriot* is such a monument in *La Comédie humaine.*

M. François Mauriac, in support of this opinion, himself adopts the parallel of towns, for he sees *Goriot* as the *rond-point* of the whole, from which radiate Balzac's

"avenues driven through the thick forests of mankind."
It has this position not only because it is the first novel in
which he used the device of recurring characters, taking
them from books that had appeared in the previous four
years, Madame de Beauséant from *La Femme abandonnée,* the Duchesse de Langeais from the story of that
name, de Marsay from *La Fille aux yeux d'or.* In *Goriot*
too are Rastignac and Bianchon, two of the most persistent and most representative figures in the whole of
La Comédie humaine, in which Rastignac appears fifteen
and Bianchon, the doctor consulted by all, no less than
twenty-three times, though here he is still a medical
student. Beyond this, *Goriot* includes Vautrin, alias
Collin, alias Herrera, alias Trompe-la-Mort, who in the
guise of a Spanish priest is to rescue Lucien from his
Illusions perdues, only to postpone his suicide until the
more terrible intrigues of *Splendeurs et misères des
courtisanes.* This is already a sufficient example of the
obsessive recurrence of figures as in a dream, where the
stories follow one another more naturally than in the
Arabian Nights.

In this sequence *Goriot* is the masterpiece of Balzac's
earlier years, as *La Cousine Bette* of the later, so the first
is naturally more concerned with a young man's entry
into life, the second with the corruption and decline of
an old one. Yet Goriot himself is an old man, as Bette's
Wenceslas is a young one—youth and age are hardly contrasts in Balzac, owing to the terrible persistence of passion. Similarly, it is not easy to trace developments or
deteriorations in his writing over the eighteen years of
his great period. There is an increased use of dialogue,
but quality and design change much less. There is not
even more cynicism or disillusion in the later work, nor
less of the romantic and the sublime, nowhere more
evident than in *Albert Savarus* or *Honorine,* both later
stories. All the changes occurred in the days of his hack-

work before he signed his name: from then he worked on *La Comédie humaine* as if it were really a single book, as if it had been present in his mind from the first novel included in it, though the earliest mention of the plan was in 1835, the year of *Goriot*'s publication.

This again is a claim for preeminence to *Goriot*, which today remains the novel available in the greatest number of different editions, after *Eugénie Grandet* which, for all its great merits, is reissued chiefly because its more innocent story is approved with less misgiving for use in schools.

Much of *Goriot* was written at Saché, in Balzac's own Touraine, where he was staying with the Margonnes, and in this retreat which relieved him of the cares, the debts, and the lures of Paris, he was able to reflect on these things. It was time for an interval, as he already had rapid experiences of success, its price and its deceptions, as he had endured the mockery of Paris and rejection by Madame de Castries. He was thirty-five, and had taken his own *Peau de chagrin* as a warning that he might die young.

In these circumstances it was natural that he should look back at Paris through the eyes of a young student, Eugène de Rastignac, innocent but ambitious, determined both to make his name and to earn enough to reward his family for the sacrifices they were making to his career. He would see the corruptions and the intrigues of Paris, but also the fascinations of its odd corners, which had attracted Balzac when he slaved in his garret near the Place de la Bastille. So Rastignac is the character most often present in *Le Père Goriot*, and most of the action concerns him.

Yet *Le Père Goriot*, as its title implies, is a study in paternity, and Goriot himself is not related to Rastignac. But Balzac, in his own Touraine and with his own experiences in mind, when conceiving a father could hardly avoid a thought of his own, who had died before his son's rise to fame—at least he gave to Goriot the same career as his father's, a commissioner of supplies to the army—though the force of paternity is more Balzac's own, in his devotion to all his characters, more especially the women, as Goriot's children were daughters.

The third great figure is Vautrin, the criminal who is so far from being the incarnation of evil that some find him the most likable person in the book—among them Madame Vauquer, who concludes even after the revelation of his crimes, "All the same, he was a good man."

In most of Balzac's novels, there is a central character who may give his or her name to the book, Eugénie Grandet, le Curé de Tours, Louis Lambert, Modeste Mignon, or la duchesse de Langeais. The title may stand for a person, as *Le Lys dans la vallée* for Henriette de Mortsauf, or in others such as *Illusions perdues*, Lucien, the disillusioned, is the central character, though unnamed in the title. Yet *Le Père Goriot* is not only the history of Goriot, for Rastignac is the central character, through whose eyes Goriot is more often seen, while it is Vautrin who precipitates the action, who is responsible for "one of the most extraordinary days in the history of the Maison Vauquer." Vautrin is likely to dominate any book, as he dominated any company in which he appeared, yet Goriot remains Balzac's best-known character, while Rastignac is central to the whole *Comédie humaine*, more frequent in his appearances than either of them, and he is followed with more interest precisely because *Goriot* gives so intimate an account of his youth.

It is a unique quality in *Goriot* that it revolves on three centres—recalling Professor Lukács's remark that "Balzac's world is, like Hegel's, a circle consisting entirely of circles." Yet the unity is complete. In some stories Balzac uses subplots skilfully integrated with the main theme, but in *Goriot* the central interest controls all the

action. Nothing is irrelevant, and the development is
closer to that of a short story than a novel. Rastignac is
directly involved with Goriot, both in defending him at
the boardinghouse and in relation to his daughter, yet
even more involved with Vautrin who tempts him with
wealth at the cost of murder.

These three are strongly contrasted characters, with
their own interests and passions, but all are intensely
Balzacian, and like most of his characters they are developed so much from inside that they are also images
of Balzac himself. Rastignac is the young Balzac in his
innocence, but also in his desire for love and fame,
Goriot is the mature Balzac sacrificing himself to the
children of his imagination (and Goriot dies calling for
his children as Balzac died asking for the doctor he had
created), while Vautrin the criminal is in a sense most
like Balzac, both in his contemptuous rejection of the
world's standards and in his imperturbable good
humour.

The three are brought together in the most natural
manner, simply because they are all staying at the same
boardinghouse on the edge of the Latin Quarter. This
is all the more natural because this Maison Vauquer, the
most famous boardinghouse in fiction or in real life, is
described in such detail and with such distaste that it
impresses its own reality on the characters before they
appear.

One trick of Balzac's technique is to concentrate on
the background to a point of exactitude that fatigues the
reader until the figures which emerge against it appear
credible, however fantastic or dramatic their behaviour.
Goriot is highly dramatic and filled with action, yet the
story has to wait until Balzac has taken nearly an eighth
of the whole book to describe the boardinghouse and
its inmates. This is not deadening, because the people
themselves are a remarkable assortment, and there is

suspense even in the description, because not only the reader but Balzac himself is eager to finish with it and begin the story. But he cannot begin until everything is ready, and tension mounts before the rising of the curtain.

These descriptions are commonly taken as realism, but they are highly personal, often dogmatic, sometimes fantastic. Balzac notes the district with some exactitude, but adds that "no part of Paris is more horrible, nor more unknown." Then the street is compared to "a bronze frame" and to the Catacombs, "withered hearts" taking the place of "empty skulls." These are not ordinary facts. The description of the sitting room is even more prejudiced, "the boardinghouse smell," the dampness and foulness, the nausea, yet all this is elegant compared with the dining room, where Balzac uses eight adjectives to indicate the decrepitude of the furniture, adding that there is no time for further details.

That is the extraordinary point, that these long descriptions are to him very hurried, and this eagerness is communicated even in the mention of furniture. His distaste and nausea are also shared, and this is important, for it stimulates interest. Why is a man such as Goriot, who has evidently been rich, who is still visited by fashionable women, living in such a place?

"Background" is hardly the word for Balzac's furniture, houses, and streets, for these are suffused with his universality of interest and constant excitement, as they are also as much a part of his characters as their clothes. In many of his works there is evidence that he saw with great intensity—he spent a couple of days in Venice, yet his *Massimilla Doni* is said by Venetians to hold the place's essence. Almost simultaneously, his interior vision peoples the place with figures, who are at once his own projections and women or men peculiar to the houses he has seen.

So the Maison Vauquer is at once a particular house in Paris and an elaborate piece of scenery for the use of Vautrin, Goriot, and Rastignac. It has to be both respectable enough for those clinging to pretensions and poor enough for those able to afford nothing better. The stairs themselves are important, for there has to be a good room on the first floor where Victorine Taillefer, the disowned daughter of a millionaire banker, can be decently lodged, and a miserable room at the top where Goriot can die without peace. Balzac sees to all this.

He sets the scene with the care of a woman who knows the sort of people coming. There is realism, there is attention to detail, but it is for their sake, not from any theory of scientific truth. That came later with the naturalism of Zola. Balzac's vision was quite undulled by any such belief that the material world was more important than the tormented or ecstatic women and men who gazed at it. Not only Goriot but Balzac himself wanted to furnish everything for his children.

Having set the scene, he relaxes with almost a sigh of relief:

> Such then was the general position at the boardinghouse at the end of the month of November, 1819. A few days later Eugène, after going to Madame de Beauséant's ball, returned at two in the morning. . . .

At the top of the stairs he notices a light under Goriot's door, opposite his own, fears the old man may be ill, peers through the keyhole, and so sees him twisting some silver plate into a solid mass. A moment later he hears Vautrin entering, though the front door has been bolted.

In this brief episode the three chief actors have been presented in character. Eugène de Rastignac is disclosed in his poverty, but also as a cousin of Madame de Beauséant, whose house is "one of the most exclusive" in Paris. At her ball he has already met the Comtesse de Restaud, who he has yet to learn is one of Goriot's two daughters. When he hears that she has been seen at the boardinghouse, then finds Goriot emerging from her house, he foolishly mentions this to her—which closes her door to him. The manner of this is typical—for she assures Rastignac that she will always be delighted to see him, then instructs her servant never to admit him.

Madame de Beauséant, his cousin, explains his blunder, adding that he had better turn to the other Goriot daughter, Delphine, married to the millionaire Baron de Nucingen.

At the boardinghouse the occasional visits of these daughters to extract the last of his money from their father (the silver plate that Rastignac had seen) have caused scandal, as nobody believes they are really his daughters. Rastignac champions him and wins his affection—Goriot even encourages his hopes with Delphine, indignant at her husband's treatment of her.

Rastignac and Goriot have much in common, for both are living in poverty, though related to the most fashionable women in Paris. Goriot is mortgaging the last of his fortune to pay his daughters' or their lovers' debts, Rastignac needs money to pay his way in a world beyond his means.

This is where Vautrin intervenes. His motives, his whole personality, remain more obscure than the others, but he is clearly indulgent towards the handsome Rastignac. Only later are his motives disclosed as both interested and perverted: "You would like to know who I am, what I've done, or what I'm doing. You are too curious, young man."

In a long talk he at least reveals his intelligence, his cynicism, his intimate understanding of Paris and the world—and not a little of Balzac's. He points out that to lead the life he wants, Rastignac needs at least a million francs, and needs them soon. Advancement in the law will get him nowhere, for he will still be a mediocrity when he is fifty. He has ambition, and Vautrin admires that. Women all turn to men of ambition, who have more strength, more blood in them, than other men.

Only two things succeed in the world, genius and corruption, because both work outside the conventions. An intelligent man has to break the conventions on a grand scale: "In every million men there are ten who put themselves above everything, even the law: and I am one of them."

He too has an ambition, to buy a plantation with a couple of hundred slaves in the United States—in ten years he will have made three or four million, but first he needs two hundred thousand francs: if he finds Rastignac a million, that is all he will ask from him.

It is very simple, for all he has to do is to court Victorine Taillefer, who already admires him. Vautrin has a man who will provoke her brother to a duel and certainly kill him with a special trick of the sword. Her father will then recognise Victorine, his only other child, and she will have a dowry of a million. There is nothing to it. Every fortune has a crime behind it—this is cleaner than most.

Rastignac recoils, but he has already seen enough of the world's hypocrisy to recognise some truth in Vautrin's talk, and even to respect his honesty. He refuses, but he is closer to corruption.

Vautrin brings out the worst in him, as Goriot brings out the best. In this, Rastignac is very much Balzac, who could understand a complete lack of scruple and a complete devotion, but found hypocrisy much harder to tolerate, for his genius made him one of those ten men in a million to whom Vautrin referred. He can describe a conventional setting, but always in terms which make it more horrible than it appears to the majority in a million men. He needed a constant stimulus (like his black coffee) as he wrote, for his vitality demanded strong emotions, and when the sublime was out of reach he had to be content with disgust. So he turned from grandeur to misery, as Rastignac from the splendid apartments of Madame de Beauséant to his garret in the Maison Vauquer.

Yet he recognised ordinary honesty, for the central point in *Goriot* is the scene in the Luxembourg gardens where Rastignac asks the advice of Bianchon, who so often in *La Comédie humaine* is the spokesman of that good sense which was Balzac's most traditional quality, the good sense of Molière. Rastignac takes an example from Rousseau: if he could become rich by killing an old mandarin in China, without stirring from Paris, would he take the chance?

Bianchon, the medical student, laughs and says that he has killed thirty-three already. But when Rastignac insists, asks him to be serious, he replies: "Is he very old, your mandarin? But all the same, whether he's young or old, paralysed or healthy, damn it . . . well, no."

He goes on to say that emotions can be as fully satisfied in a small sphere as in a great one. Napoleon could not enjoy the same meal twice, nor more mistresses than a student. Happiness, whether it cost a million or a hundred, was still limited to one person's capacity for enjoyment.

This brief exchange in the Luxembourg gardens, so typical of a medical student's outer cynicism and inner good faith, helps Rastignac to resist Vautrin's offer. These interventions of good sense in a temptation or a passion are often brief in Balzac, and as often made by a minor character, yet they have the same force of a lapse from extravagance into wisdom as occurs in his master, Rabelais.

As Rastignac goes more into the world and becomes

more involved with Goriot's daughter Delphine, his need of money grows more pressing until one evening, almost without thinking, he makes himself agreeable to the heiress Victorine—but it is not with his consent that Vautrin carries out his scheme, and on her brother's death, her father sends for her. On the same morning, Vautrin is arrested, not for this crime (which remains unsuspected as he had promised) but because his identity as an escaped criminal has been unearthed by the police.

The police officer remarks that Vautrin is not interested in women, and he had once gone to prison for a crime really committed by a handsome young Italian. Evidently he is a homosexual—Balzac noted such facts, and the Lesbian Marquise in *La Fille aux yeux d'or* in the century before Gide or Proust, without their emphasis, but as an aspect of the corrupt society whose secretary he was. Vautrin interested him more as a critic of that society, for he shared his view that more harm was done by bankers, such as Nucingen and Taillefer, than by thieves or murderers. Yet it would be difficult to say that he judged even misers or millionaires harshly, for he was so inside his characters that he judged them with their own self-pity.

Most of all, he was inside Goriot, in his obsession with his daughters, which is at once obviously morbid and deeply moving, because it is a real and basically natural devotion for which he makes very real sacrifices. They have had nearly all his great fortune, they refuse to be seen with him in public, yet he continues to adore them, and stands with the crowds outside the Opera simply to catch a glimpse of them.

Vautrin casts his great shadow over the book, all the more sinister in his genial good nature, but his arrest removes him three-quarters of the way through—when Rastignac, in horror at the crime in which he has so nearly taken part, abandons every thought of Victorine, now an heiress, and turns with all the more passion towards Delphine, as if this affair with a banker's wife was sacred by contrast. This brings him still closer to Goriot, whose illness, madness, and death dominate the last quarter of the book, earning his right to the title.

In Vautrin, Rastignac has seen the effect of strong intelligence, uncontrolled by scruple or emotion. In Goriot, he now sees the effect of devotion and feelings equally uncontrolled. Both impress him, but the end of Goriot moves him more deeply because he is in love with one of the two daughters whose alternate bleeding and neglect of their father bring him to that end.

The final blow falls when both daughters come to him for money and he has none left:

> This is death to me . . . but what will become of you when I'm no longer here? Fathers should live as long as their children. God, how badly organized your world is! Yet you too have a son, so they tell us. You should prevent us from suffering in our children.

Then, more terribly, the two daughters have a violent quarrel in his presence which so strikes the principle of his life, divided wholly between them, that he collapses. Bianchon is summoned, and concludes from a glance at the eyes that there has been a stroke with a threat of apoplexy.

The daughters having gone, he and Rastignac look after the old man, until Rastignac is called away by Delphine whom he had promised to take to Madame de Beauséant's last reception on which she had set her heart (only he had been able to secure her an invitation). At the ball he says that her father's last cry is in his ears, at which she sheds a tear, hastily brushed aside with the thought that it will ruin her makeup.

After the ball, he returns to Goriot's bedside, to hear

the last great tirade and rhapsody over his daughters. As
the end is obviously near, Rastignac sends for them, but
they fail to appear.

Goriot at last brings to the front the reflections which
have been tormenting the back of his mind:

> They have their affairs, they are asleep, they won't come.
> . . . You give them life, they give you death. You make their
> way in the world, they chase you from it. No, they won't
> come. I've known that for ten years . . . but I wouldn't
> believe it.

For the first time, the bitterness of truth invades him,
as he realises that if he had been less devoted, if he had
kept his fortune, they would be there at his bedside. He
recalls how they once were—even when they were first
married, he was welcome at their houses, then gradually
his presence embarrassed them, and he stayed away for
their sake:

> That's what it is to educate your children well. Yet I
> couldn't go to school, not at my age . . . this agony—let the
> doctors open my head, that would hurt less. My daughters,
> my daughters . . . send the police for them, justice is on my
> side, nature, the law, everything. The fatherland depends
> on fathers and will go under with them. That's obvious.
> Society, the whole world, turns on fatherhood. Everything's
> upset if children don't care for their fathers. Oh, just to
> see them . . . and tell them not to look at me so coldly
> when they come.

Then his mind revolves the other way: they are innocent, and it is all his fault, because he has spoiled them.
God would be unjust to condemn them for his sake.
He will make more millions, to bring them back. Then
again: "I'm a fool. They don't love me, they've never
loved me. It's all clear now. They won't come."

When Rastignac says he will fetch them, Goriot tells
him to make the government, the king's officer, act

against them. Reminded that he has cursed them, he is astonished: no, he loves, adores them, and he would be cured if they came. A moment later he demands "a law on the death of fathers."

Rastignac goes off to bring the daughters, but the most he can achieve is a promise from Delphine that she will come, and this is given more for his sake than her father's. When he returns, the end is already near. As he and Bianchon are changing the old man's sheets and lifting him up, he grasps their hair and cries, "Ah, my angels," dying with a sigh of relief at this last illusion.

In a few minutes a woman's step is heard outside. Rastignac at once says, "She has come too late." But it is not Delphine, only the maid to explain why she can't come.

It is by such touches that Balzac skirts convention and arrives at the more fantastic cruelty in life.

It remains only to bury Goriot, which is not easy as there is no money left, and both sons-in-law refuse appeals to them.

Bianchon proposes an epitaph:

> Here lies M. Goriot, father of the Comtesse de Restaud and Baronne de Nucingen, buried at the expense of two students.

Goriot has a pauper's funeral, with Rastignac as the only mourner. Looking down on Paris from the cemetery, he sees the world he has to conquer, and issues his challenge, "*À nous deux maintenant.*"

Balzac himself had already advanced into the centre of his world when in 1835 he published *Le Père Goriot*, for it was one of his most productive years in which also appeared *Séraphita* and *Le Lys dans la vallée*, both major works, as well as *Le Contrat de mariage*, a shorter novel. So he had already delivered himself of those books which weigh on a writer more from a necessity of deliverance from them than from his own vision, whether they are the expression of his youth, such as *Louis Lambert* and *Le Lys dans la vallée,* a statement of a political position such as *Le Médecin de campagne,* or a statement of religion such as *Séraphita.* He had even expressed his whole vision of life in *La Peau de chagrin.*

In *Le Père Goriot* he attained what is for many a greater achievement, the direct creation of life. Goriot, Vautrin, Rastignac are figures more clearly defined than Balzac himself, for he shaped them with a greater art than he gave to his daily life, in which he was often content to indulge his imagination—and this caused fantastic episodes which some found inconsistent with his genius. But when he wrote he was himself: Goriot is consistent, even if Balzac is not.

It is true that both Goriot and Vautrin are extraordinary creations: Goriot is the genius of fatherhood ("the Christ of paternity" to Rastignac) as Vautrin is the genius of crime, but they are consistent and impose conviction. It is only in *Le Père Goriot* that Balzac put two such characters in a single novel, and this sometimes creates a strange effect, as a sudden passing from light into darkness. Yet this strengthens more than it weakens the theme of the book, which is based on contrasts between success and failure, riches and poverty, devotion and indifference. But Balzac was doubtless wise to arrest and remove Vautrin before Goriot's greatest scenes: so terrible a passion required the whole stage.

For *Le Père Goriot* remains the bible of fatherhood, and so it is inevitably compared with *King Lear.* Clearly the poetry and the grandeur of Shakespeare triumph, but in one not unimportant particular Goriot has an advantage over Lear, in that he is more human. He is driven out of his mind only after his stroke, and even then he rallies, sees that he is himself much to blame, that he has spoiled his daughters. These daughters themselves are human, not monsters such as Goneril and Regan. Delphine especially has not only charm but moments of tenderness which make it easy to share Rastignac's fondness for her. Goriot's daughters are simply women with social cares and worries over money: they would come to his death-bed if only he had chosen to die at a more convenient time, and they are genuinely upset when they learn of their failure. Delphine even said, "I would be a monster if I did not come." But she is not a monster, only a woman preoccupied, and in letting this be seen Balzac adds that extra dimension of tragedy represented by the words, "If only. . . ."

Le Père Goriot retains a special place in La Comédie humaine because, unlike some pieces which are chiefly interesting in their relation to the whole, this with half-a-dozen others support that whole which without them would fall to pieces.

4

Physiology of Woman

BALZAC INVENTED SO MANY WOMEN and in such variety that they are his chief claim to creative vision, for if it is true that he is also inside them, this is a much greater achievement than the projection of himself inside creatures of his own gender. That he is inside these women has nowhere been better asserted than in the great phrase of Henry James:

> He bears children with Madame de l'Estorade, knows intimately how she suffers for them, and not less intimately how her correspondent suffers, as well as enjoys, without them. Big as he is, he makes himself small to be handled by her with young maternal passion, and positively to handle her in turn with infantile innocence.

This is all the more remarkable because he hardly received attention from his own mother, and had very little home life. His first knowledge of women as so much else came to him from Madame de Berny. Yet she was certainly not the only woman from whom he learned— these lines of Henry James were written of *Mémoires de deux jeunes mariées* which Marcel Bouteron believes were influenced by Balzac's correspondence with the Countess Guidoboni-Visconti. He corresponded with many other women, even apart from Zulma Carraud and

Madame Hanska, who after years of correspondence became his wife. He once told Gautier that for a writer affairs were best conducted by letter, as this helped to form the style.

In some of these letters he gave the impression that he worked in monastic solitude and may even have believed this at the moment of writing, for he was no less a monk than he was, when impersonating Vautrin, a criminal. He certainly believed that continence preserved the energy necessary for his work, though the Goncourts' story that he lamented on emerging from a woman's embrace, "I have lost a book," is probably only a well-found illustration of this principle. In fact the principle was violated, and he "knew women" in the scriptural sense no less than he knew them by letters.

His sister, in her memoir of him, notes with some amusement the efforts he made to óbserve discretion about his affairs. This discretion was not always proof, in exuberant moments, against mysterious allusions to women of immense distinction who had been with him. Anyhow, the efforts directed against gossip have proved vain against scholars and critics, who have done worse than any scandalmongers in revealing his private life. Nor is their work unrewarding when it helps to clarify the intimate understanding of women displayed in *La Comédie humaine*, where he invented so many.

Yet the strange impression that a student of Balzac has, on making the acquaintance of these real women he knew, is that he also invented them. Art seems once more to have anticipated life. His passion and his gratitude for Madame de Berny, a woman twice his age, whose children were closer in years to him, are less easy to believe than some affairs in his novels to which he has given the deeper reality of his own vision. His bitter despair over Madame de Castries is harder to understand than Montriveau's over the Duchesse de Langeais, whose charms are more convincing. Most certainly his affair with Madame Hanska, ending with their marriage and his death, is more astonishing than any improbabilities in *Albert Savarus,* the novel in which he described its course without knowing its end. Truth here is really stranger than fiction.

Yet it is also true that these women bear some responsibility for the fiction. Art reverses the roles of physical creation, for women provide the seed that enables a Balzac to give birth to his characters. It may even be argued that if there had been no Madame de Berny, he would have created no such women characters, or at least they would have been different—for a man whose work was so feminine in substance was predestined to a woman. In being that woman, the first in his life, she not only inspired those in his work, but those he was to meet after her, for most of them were women of distinction, her equal or superior in status and elegance, having her literary interests and knowledge of the world, holding her religious and royalist opinions, even encumbered as she was with a difficult or disagreeable husband, offering in fact exactly the qualities and the situation that Balzac had found in her.

It has been remarked that, to a man, the women he loves are always the same woman, because what he finds in them is an image of his own desire. To an imagination on the scale of a Balzac this certainly applies, and the best women in his work—in which women more often behave better than men—and in his life bear a certain resemblance to Madame de Berny, because they would not have attracted him nor taken his time if they had lacked that essential quality.

In his earlier work she is assigned the role of the "angelic" or "sublime" woman who sacrifices herself for a man and consoles him in his labours. Both in *La Peau de chagrin* and *Louis Lambert* she has this role

(Pauline), but a fuller account of their relationship is in *Le Lys dans la vallée,* published in 1835, the year before her death, where she appears as Henriette de Mortsauf.

Like *Louis Lambert* this work is more impressive as a wonderful evocation of youth than as a novel, though here the interest is much stronger. The enchanted spring of Touraine and the wonder of Félix de Vandenesse, hardly more than a boy, in his first worship of a woman, are distilled in the sunshine of these pages, where Balzac describes the fields and flowers with the same impatient eagerness as he gives to the misery of the Maison Vauquer at the beginning of *Goriot.* Even the startling incident when Félix first sees Henriette sitting in front of him in a corner at a dance and kisses her bare back, at which she turns angrily and sees a boy with a tear trickling down his face, even this can be treated with her own indulgence, because it is obvious that not only he, but Balzac, could not help it.

It is absurd, but it presents the right balance between the boldness and the timidity of a first affair, for if Balzac's women or men are sometimes extravagant in their conduct or language, they are always human—they exaggerate only what really happens. *Le Lys dans la vallée* becomes less convincing precisely when Balzac, out of devotion to Madame de Berny, departs from what really happened. For in the book he not only makes her as noble and selfless as she doubtless was, but shows her treating Félix as a son and giving no return to his love, only admitting her own for him when she lies dying. Yet she bitterly repents this love—disproportionate in her though less in Madame de Berny, as she had sacrificed the whole of her reputation and some part of her children's fortune to Balzac. So the angel of the sublime, who was always his evil spirit, intervened in the story to weaken it.

Félix himself undergoes a similar change, for when he

leaves Henriette and falls to the fantastic Lady Dudley, this appears to be the consequence of Henriette's austerity, yet in reality Madame de Berny had been less austere, and Balzac had been even less faithful than Félix. His first years of success had been celebrated by affairs with women who continued his education from the elements supplied by her. In *Le Lys dans la vallée* he showed his gratitude by ascribing that education wholly to her, but in reality he learned much from others.

Not least among them was this Lady Dudley, only less fantastic than the real Countess Guidoboni-Visconti whose acquaintance he had made at the Austrian Embassy in Paris. She was English by birth, a Sarah Lovell from an eccentric family in Kent—Lady Dudley came from Lancashire "where women die of love." On the Countess its effect was less fatal: she had married an Italian count who had dissipated his youth until nothing was left but a passion for music (*Massimilla Doni* gives some indication of this), and his chief delight was to play second fiddle in a theatre orchestra. The Countess also consoled herself: Lady Dudley remarks in *Une Fille d'Ève*, "One exists with a husband, one only lives with a lover." Balzac once escaped from his creditors by taking refuge in the house of the Viscontis, which led to the husband being sued for his debts—one more situation more proper to *La Comédie humaine* than to real life.

The charm of the Countess for Balzac was that she shared his enjoyment of escapades and defiance of conventions, being one of those Englishwomen who, once freed from British restraints, become more exuberant than any southerner on the Continent. Balzac's references to English hypocrisy—"Speak to a woman . . . pay a compliment . . . shocking . . . shocking"—owe something to the force of her own reaction against it.

Balzac wrote *Le Lys dans la vallée* as a tribute to Madame de Berny, but also to explain his relations with her to Madame Hanska, which was another reason why these had to be raised to a higher level in the book. The letter at the beginning from Félix to Natalie de Manerville sets out his devotion, while her letter at the end, telling him that women are not very interested in the woman who came before them, may represent Madame Hanska's reaction.

It was a different woman who gave him some of the material for the very different book, *Physiologie du mariage*, with which he had earlier made his name. He had met the Duchesse d'Abrantès when he was still engaged in hackwork, as she, widow of Napoleon's General Junot, had also been reduced to this. She was able to tell him all the scandals of Napoleon's court, where the Emperor himself had been at least among her admirers. In the preface of *Physiologie du mariage* Balzac refers to her as one of the wittiest women of her age, and with his gift for absorbing the experiences of women proceeds to write as if he had intimate knowledge of marital crises.

The form and style of the book obviously owe much to Brillat-Savarin's *Physiologie du goût*, which had appeared only five years before, with its maxims and its meditations, and there is even something of the same mock-heroic manner. Beyond that, there are eighteenth century influences hardly less obvious, for Balzac here is at his least romantic—in all his work, if he mentions Rousseau, the prototype of the romantic, it is usually to disagree with him, while Diderot, the type of rationalism and encyclopaedism, is quoted with respect. *Physiologie du mariage* even has some claim to be an encyclopaedic work, for very few of the misfortunes to be encountered in marriage are neglected. There are one or two references to its joys, but Balzac is here most concerned to warn husbands against the dangers to which they are exposed—warnings which M. de Berny, M. Visconti, and M. Hanski might well have taken to heart. He even offers statistics of those who are unmarried and likely to disrupt the peace of homes.

While exposing the tricks by which women deceive the men who have disappointed them, he places the blame on the men. He anticipates the work of later psychologists in emphasizing the delicacy necessary to love: "Never begin a marriage with a rape." This famous maxim is typical, for here as in his stories he was the defender of women against the brutality and stupidity of men.

He explains how French society had reached an unsatisfactory compromise between Roman subjection and Frankish independence for women, resulting in that situation where unmarried women were almost an enclosed order, married women even more at the mercy of their lovers than their husbands. Love and marriage were in fact dissociated. Balzac claimed that the greater freedom enjoyed by girls in Switzerland or in English-speaking lands offered a better chance of happiness. It is noteworthy that in his own novels two of the few girls who achieve happiness in marriage, Modeste Mignon and Ursule Mirouet, both have an enlightened father or guardian who allows them to make their own choice.

Physiologie du mariage describes the misfortunes of marriage with gaiety, even with cynicism—it shocked Parisians on its appearance—but Balzac was no more indifferent to marriage than Brillat-Savarin to food, though he wrote as lightly. Marriage extends beyond the kitchen, but he wrote no less rationally of honeymoons and double beds than his predecessor of chocolate and truffles. There is much good sense, yet also a lyrical passage on that true love which is a direct gift of the gods.

If some of the basic wisdom came from Madame de Berny and some of the anecdotes from the Duchesse d'Abrantès, he had a deep insight into women's feelings, and the stories that followed often apply the lessons of

Physiologie du mariage. La Femme abandonnée may
have been inspired by the Duchesse herself, but Madame
de Berny had shown him what a woman could suffer.
He exalted her again in *Madame Firmiani* (which he
tactfully dedicated to her husband), while in *La Femme
de trente ans* he showed the unhappy course of a woman
with a characterless husband such as hers.

Most of Balzac's women express themselves in their
love, whether this is sacrificial, devoted, passionate, or
mercenary. But there are some who are too proud or too
cold to love, though they take a pride in being loved, and
may even encourage passions which they have no inten-
sion of sharing. For these he had a model in Henriette,
later Duchesse de Castries, who first wrote to him in the
year of his success with *La Peau de chagrin*. She pre-
tended to be an English admirer of his, and he was
excited both by this proof of his fame abroad and by
the quality of the writing paper, which was the first
clue to her distinction. When the time came for her to
reveal her identity, he was much more excited, as she was
the great lady of his imagination, and her uncle, the
Duc de Fitzjames, was the leader of the legitimist party.
Her chief object was probably to secure a brilliant young
writer for that cause.

If, as he later declared, this was the most bitter experience of Balzac's life, his disappointment was not only in
her, for he was also disillusioned with himself, with the
woman of his imagination, with the aristocracy, with the
royalist cause, and even with his hopes for France. For
Madame de Castries embodied not only his illusions, but
some of his principles—these survived her, but they were
modified by doubts on the aristocracy which professed
them. Later in *Le Cabinet des antiques* (the nickname
of a diehard group) he showed how powerless they were
to alter the course of events, as in *Les Paysans* they were

superseded even on their estates by speculators from the towns.

In the autumn of 1832 he travelled with Madame de Castries and her uncle to Aix-les-Bains and Geneva, a journey which revealed to him that she was as unlikely to favour him as her party was to govern France. Over a year later he expressed his deception in her treatment of him with *La Duchesse de Langeais,* which resembles *Le Lys dans la vallée* in convincing more when it keeps to the facts than when it exaggerates and sublimates them. Balzac could magnificently transform a real woman or boardinghouse and raise them into the other world of art—it was only his own fantastic experience that he was unable to control. His assault on Madame de Castries was basically as fantastic as Montriveau's attempt to kidnap the Duchesse de Langeais from a convent off the coast of Spain after she had become a nun. The detail and the description of the convent are admirable, the rocky islet with the palm trees above the gleaming waters of the Mediterranean where women from all over Europe came to enter the strictest of the Carmelite orders. But Montriveau's long search ending in his interview with the nun there is only less fantastic than the last coincidence when he scales the cliff, finds her laid out for burial while the sisters are in choir, and elopes with her corpse.

Yet it is with great art that Balzac begins and ends the story in the convent, taking only a few pages for this, while he places in between the whole affair of the Duchesse and Montriveau. He is subtle in analysis of her pride, her coquetry and her refusal, her desire to make the conquest of a great man whose simplicity of heart she admires, her fear of compromising her own position. Behind this is another contrast between the arrogant conventions of the old regime which she represents and the simple directness of a Bonapartist general—or between Henriette and the Napoleonic directness of Balzac.

In the last analysis the affair is projected with a vision of such power that the exaggeration of the convent scenes at the beginning and end no longer seems absurd, for they embody the real exaltations and frustrations of a grand passion. It is not true that Henriette entered an enclosed order, but it is true that she was enclosed in the rigidity of her own conventions. It is not true that Balzac kidnapped her corpse from the convent, but it is true that she raised him to that frenzy of desperation.

The story is typical of Balzac, who forces belief by the accuracy of his detail and his analysis of personal relations, who then intensifies his vision to a depth where the reader is startled to observe strange and unknown creatures beneath a sea as familiar as that Mediterranean in which the Duchesse de Langeais had her convent.

This meeting of reality and vision is even more remarkable in the affair of Eveline Hanska. She too introduced herself (in 1832) with a letter under an assumed name, *l'Étrangère,* aided by her child's Swiss governess, who afterwards had scruples on the part she played in the affair. To Madame Hanska, immured with a husband much older than herself in a vast Palladian mansion in the Ukraine, the arrival of novels and papers from Paris was the chief excitement of life. Balzac was no less excited when he learned that his correspondent was really a Polish countess, one of whose great-greataunts had been Anne Leczinska, Queen of France.

The affair was obviously more suited to romantic fiction than to real life, and the fact that he met her the following year at Neuchâtel and also at Geneva, that the letters continued, that they married eighteen years after the first letter, has its chief interest to the critic in the effect on his work.

Some items in *La Comédie humaine,* among them

Séraphita, Modeste Mignon, Albert Savarus, Honorine, are directly related to Balzac's devotion to Madame Hanska. All may be charged with sublimity or romanticism, yet it is difficult for a critic to say that they present situations impossible in real life, when they are often less fantastic than Balzac's own experience.

In every period the style of the day affects the language and even the behaviour of lovers, but it is even more understandable that a writer as creative as Balzac should extend his conceptions from literature into life. This point is capital in justice to Madame Hanska and to her influence on his life and writings. Writers sympathetic to Balzac, among them Dr. Herbert J. Hunt, the best of recent critics in English, have viewed this influence with regret, feeling that she imposed on him eighteen years of frustration. Such a view has authority, and it is at least evident that this long affair denied him the peace and serenity of married life.

Yet domestic peace, or indeed peace of any sort, may not be the need most urgent to the temperament of a Balzac. What he most needed was the renewal of those visions and illusions which he translated into his words and work. In this, frustration itself was an aid, as it is the unsatisfied lover who writes the most passionate declarations.

That Balzac realised this is proved by his effort to live as a monk, his monastic robe, his abstinence—he ate and drank very frugally, apart from his vast infusions of coffee, while at work, though he feasted during breaks in his labours. By concentration and willpower, which he believed was the impulse of all thought (that was the basis of both Louis Lambert's and Raphael's Treatise on the Will) he hoped to lead a purely intellectual life, and he at least succeeded in the slavery of his work. Even when he was writing love letters or pursuing an affair it was a point of honour with him not to steal time from his working hours: he preferred to sacrifice his sleep and his health.

This was not the life of a husband—indeed any sensible woman, such as Zulma Carraud, prescribed as a wife for him, would have been the first to protest, and rightly, at such a life. Nor is it true that Madame Hanska destroyed his domestic peace, for if he loved her he had an immense capacity for loving, and there were other women (he was not faithful to her through all those years of separation). The truth was that he preferred the vision which she represented in his mind, and it was from that vision that he created some of his most hallucinating figures.

Madame Hanska was in fact largely the creation of Balzac, as he was himself formed by Madame de Berny, and it is in these two women that his perceptions were at once inspired and embodied, so that the women of *La Comédie humaine* are directly related to them, either as sisters or daughters. Yet the effect they had on him was so strongly marked by his own temperament and reactions that it is impossible to distinguish exactly between their reality and his own vision of them. Between them, too, stands the figure of Madame de Castries who in the mythology of Mr. Robert Graves might be described as "the white goddess," personifying a fate in the alteration of a man's life. Yet even she had already been represented as Fedora, "the woman without a heart" in *La Peau de chagrin,* precisely the novel which had attracted her to Balzac.

All three women can be discerned in the vision of *La Comédie humaine,* to which Madame de Berny gives the indulgence and devotion of women, Madame de Castries their pride and inaccessibility, while Madame Hanska embodies something more exotic, the woman to whom a man aspires though baulked by all the difficulties

—distance, social position, poverty, or husbands—that stand in his way.

The name chosen by her, *l'Étrangère,* emphasizes this quality. She was the foreigner in a wider sense than the English term, as she was also the woman who remains always strange in a man's experience, belonging to the other world, even if this be only the other world of women, and in many of Balzac's novels this is their first attraction to men, who in their cliché-ridden existence need the stimulus of the one refreshing cliché, the woman who is "different."

Madame de Berny and Madame Hanska deserve their special place in Balzac's life because they both realised that he was "different"—in his genius—from other men. Madame de Berny had the greater part of nursing and inspiring that genius, which Madame Hanska respected more than the man in whom it had—awkwardly or even grossly—assumed flesh (she was shaken at their first meeting by his manners at table).

Yet Madame Hanska may have been all the more valuable to him in her insistence on his fame as a writer and on her own role as *l'Étrangère.* The strangest product of this influence was *Séraphita,* which he wrote at her request, a book considered by some to be his least characteristic—they even resent its inclusion in *La Comédie humaine.* Others, among whom was Yeats, find it his most interesting work, the one in which his vision is most free. *Séraphita* is in fact a crux of Balzac criticism: whether he is regarded as most himself in that or in *Eugénie Grandet* has a similar importance to analysing Dickens in *Hard Times* or in *The Pickwick Papers.* In Dickens the poles are the grim and the comic, in Balzac the vision and the reality.

Such easy contrasts are more often a temptation than an aid, for they weaken the personality of a writer whose greatness is precisely the breadth and unity of his work. *Séraphita* and *Eugénie Grandet* spring from the same jet of imagination, however wide its range, for the Norwegian background of *Séraphita* is even more definite than the details of Saumur, though Balzac had never been to Norway and Saumur was only just beyond his own Touraine.

The mysticism of *Séraphita* was more closely related to the loves and passions of *La Comédie humaine* than may be apparent to those who question its right there, for the seraphic figure who appeared to a woman as Séraphitus, to a man as Séraphita, illuminates not only divine love as expounded by Swedenborg, but human love as conceived by Balzac. *Séraphita* may be an angelic figure, but that brings her all the closer to Henriette de Mortsauf, to Adeline Hulot, to Madame de la Chanterie and all the other "sublime" or "angelic" creatures of Balzac's world.

Because he had this exalted conception of love, expressed most fully in *Séraphita,* he imagined women who passed naturally from the love of a man to love of God. Owing to this, the Duchesse de Langeais, once passion has been aroused in her but not satisfied, enters a convent, as Véronique Graslin, after a man has died for her, devotes herself to good works directed by the abbé Bonnet (*Le Curé de village*), as Adeline Hulot, deserted by the husband she worships, dedicates herself to the poor of Paris. Even women who sell themselves are no less readily transformed into worshippers, as Esther developes piety in her convent, as Coralie dies in an aura of devotion, as even Valérie Marneffe, the most cynical of Balzac's women, sets herself to win treasure in heaven when she no longer has any use for that she has accumulated on earth.

These transformations are doubtless also the trick of a novelist, yet suicide would be an even more striking trick, but Balzac's women are above that, which comes more naturally to the weak and selfish Lucien. The women really make a religion of love—"the most beautiful of human religions," as Albert Savarus, modelled on Balzac himself, refers to it.

This exalted conception of love, particularly of women's love, was largely responsible for the immense popularity of his novels with women—and especially with Madame Hanska. He received so many letters from women that he was unable to answer them all himself and handed some over to Zulma Carraud, who once by mistake answered one from Madame Hanska. Balzac passed over the difference in handwriting by explaining that under the strain of work his writing changed to suit the character. More ingeniously he explained a letter discovered by M. Hanski as being written on a laughing challenge from his wife to see if he could manage a love letter as well as a novel. In fact he had plenty of practice in both.

If he sometimes appears too fluent in passion, both in novels and letters, this is only because it came so naturally to him, both in practice and on principle, for "passion is the whole of humanity." This was not a typically romantic exaggeration, for it was Balzac himself who set the style. He was not simply following a romantic tradition, as the chief influence before him was Walter Scott, whose women are very different from Diane de Maufrigneuse or la Torpille. Balzac was not even following a tradition in France, where emphasis in the age before him had been more on the pleasure than the passion of love. As the old baron in *Madame Firmiani* declared, "We only made love—today you love." Balzac was not of course alone in this, as the Revolution had altered the expression of feeling, but George Sand was more representative of that by insisting on the freedom to love. Balzac in principle disagreed with her: he believed in love, but he also believed in marriage—a delicate position which he was not alone in finding difficult to maintain.

Yet the passion with which he devoted himself to *l'Étrangère*, to reconcile love and marriage at the end, if only at the cost of his life, proves the seriousness with which he wrote *Séraphita* (even while its heaviness proved that his real genius was for fantasy or comedy). He dedicated it to Madame Hanska as:

> . . . one of those balustrades carved by an artist strong in faith on which pilgrims lean while contemplating the choir of some great church and meditating on the end of man.

Balzac and Madame Hanska belonged to the same physical type, dark and plump, inclined to exuberance in body and temperament. But they had no less a common impulse towards the supernatural, especially in the form of mysterious and "magnetic" attractions. This corner of Balzac's mind was ignored in the last century, as it was unwelcome either to the rationalism or to the religion of his readers, until in 1899 Dr. Augustin Cabanès published his *Balzac ignoré*. But it is still too often dismissed as the foible of a writer who otherwise had an almost scientific sense of reality. It is true that Balzac had a strong interest in science, but this was precisely on its more esoteric side, and he was most fascinated by the physiognomy of Lavater and the phrenology of Gall, not today viewed as the most respectable of the sciences, and his own use of the term is most frequent in references to "the occult sciences."

It is not only *Séraphita* that reveals this: there is the case of Dr. Minoret in *Ursule Mirouet*, the fortuneteller in *Le Cousin Pons*, the extraordinary "magnetic" strength displayed by Madame de Sérizy in *Splendeurs et misères des courtisanes*—and these things, far from being romantic or fictional machinery, are offered as serious observation. Balzac was in fact more attracted, even as an observer, by phenomena that could not be explained rationally than by rational reductions of them. He would have agreed with Giraudoux that "the direction of our lives achieves certainty by virtue of our ignorance, not by our explanations."

For Balzac this ignorance, whose secrets are today more commonly assigned to the unconscious, was enveloped in the occult sciences, and at the head of them was the mysticism which he expressed in *Séraphita*. It was natural that Madame Hanska should demand this of him and that he should dedicate it to her, because this celestial love was the best they could achieve when she was incarcerated with her husband in the Ukraine, but their occult science was also of value to them as a means of communication in a shared belief, a nourishment to their hopes.

With other women of that generation, Madame Hanska had a desire for emotional and artistic sustenance, for recognition too of their own sensitivity to feeling and to art. It was a movement of feminism that raised the position of women by insisting on the value of intuition and mysteries of feeling which could themselves border on the occult, as some of their secrets and charms came close to witchcraft. Balzac shared this belief in such exaltations of feeling, not only the heights he revealed in *Séraphita* but even the minor crises of nerves, as in *Étude de femme*. He had a woman's sense that the personal is more important than the political, that it was "more human to obey friendship than tyrannical laws," as in the Preface to *La Comédie humaine* he asserted that "the battle waged in the Indre valley between Madame de Mortsauf and passion may be as great as the most famous of recorded battles."

He was not trying to sublimate these feminine crises,

for in his eyes their sufferings were already "sublime." He judged them simply by their consequences, as in *Mémoires de deux jeunes mariées* he showed that Renée, who sacrificed her life to her husband and children, in the end achieved a greater happiness and satisfaction than Louise, who gave all to love, exhausting both her husbands, the first by the tyranny of her de- mands on him, the second by the almost greater tyranny of her gifts to him. Yet Louise—the novel is told in letters between the two who had been girls at the same convent—writes with even more truth and passion than Renée: life itself divides their destinies, not Balzac who, as Henry James noted, is no less intimately present in the one than in the other.

Here again he is both less romantic and less revolu- tionary than George Sand, who regarded love as an absolute value above any claim of marriage or society (they once had an argument on this point which lasted most of the night). But he realised no less clearly the anguish of passion under social or moral restraints, and his vision of this was so intense that he was often accused of encouraging it.

This charge was hardly just, for his vision was essen- tially feminine, as he shared both the feeling of women that love was "the key to higher worlds" (*Séraphita*) and their equal certainty that children and homes were the most important elements of this one (*Mémoires de deux jeunes mariées*). Obviously there is a discrepancy between these views which can only issue in conflicts and crises, to provide most of literature's material, not only Balzac's—the originality of his vision was that it was double, equally intense in both aspects, less limited than idealism or cynicism which both ignore one aspect. If there is a contradiction in this view, it remains a human outlook with two eyes. Later naturalism closed one eye, with a microscopic effect in contrast to Balzac's magnifying power.

For all his feminine vision, which accorded so well with an intuition often regarded as irrational in a world of masculine values, he remained very much a man subject to the stresses of his own passions. If Madame Hanska was his Séraphita, he found it more difficult to be her Séraphitus. A cartoon showing the monk and his angel carousing together draw attention to this. Madame Hanska and his women readers who so quickly identified themselves with his sublime or nobly passionate heroines protested against the entry of some others into his work, not only the scandalous Impéria of the *Contes drolatiques*, but such ones as Jenny Cadine, Carabine, la Torpille, Suzanne de Valadon, Coralie, and the *lorettes* who made their living out of men in *La Comédie humaine* itself.

These women were neither sublime nor angelic, yet Balzac's vision of them had an indulgence that was more masculine than feminine, for what he most emphasizes is their generosity. They too are much better than the men who make use of them. At times they even offer examples to other women, as Josépha in *La Cousine Bette* says that the government ought to set up gymnastic classes to teach virtuous women the art of handling their men, for to her the devoted Adeline Hulot seems pitifully ignorant.

Women such as Carabine or Coralie who gave themselves to artists and journalists while selling themselves to bankers had a quick intelligence and acquired a wider knowledge than the arts of love. They even became expert hostesses or presided over Bohemian dinners at the Rocher de Cancale where Balzac made their acquaintance—among them was Olympe Pelissier who married Rossini. They had qualities not to be found in Balzac's duchesses, and some find the Jennys and the Carabines more attractive than his countesses.

To Balzac with his ardour and sympathy for women of all sorts, their attractions were all-triumphant when he was writing of them—with the passion of Louise determined to find a lover worthy of her the moment she is out of her convent, or with the devotion of Renée writing letters in reply to her closest friend. Nor were the duchesses always so different from the Carabines, for Diane de Maufrigneuse, later Princesse de Cadignan, disguises herself as a man and goes posting down to Alençon to get her lover out of a scrape—an escapade bold enough for any *lorette*. Yet, for all these gay inventions Balzac is never happier than in his creation of girlhood, though he admitted the difficulty: "To create many virgins requires the genius of a Raphael."

Eugénie Grandet, Modeste Mignon, Ursule Mirouet, Césarine Birotteau, Pauline, Pierette, these and other virgins have less monotony than those of Raphael. The remarkable thing about all these girls is that they are much less often deceived than the women of the world, the countesses and the duchesses. Their innocence is clearer than the obscure results of experience. If they have illusions, these quickly vanish when they inspect the man of their choice more closely. Eugénie Grandet has dreams of her Charles until she discovers his acquisitive nature, when she gives him money but refuses herself to him. Modeste Mignon rejects Canalis, the writer whose poetic style she has so much admired, for the same reason.

Modeste Mignon, published only six years before Balzac's death, is a light comedy with a happy ending, rare in *La Comédie humaine*. It was dedicated to a "polonaise," obviously Madame Hanska, in phrases attributing to her all the charms of innocence and experience. There is a Ferdinand and Miranda relationship between Modeste and her Ernest, with her father playing the role of a Prospero, and the book has the serenity of a *Tempest*: even the father's recovery of fortune and title bears out the parallel. The difference is that it was not an ultimate work, for *Les Parents pauvres* was still to come. But it shows how Balzac might have developed if he had achieved earlier the happy marriage which he there imagines, for it was written after the death of Count Hanski, at the time when other obstacles in the way of marriage seemed less considerable than they proved to be. Admirable though it is, there is little cause for regret. Others could write light pieces, but not a *Goriot* or an *Illusions perdues*.

In *Les Secrets de la princesse de Cadignan,* published five years before *Modeste Mignon,* he had created a more sophisticated comedy which had a happy ending of a different sort. Here Diane de Maufrigneuse who had numbered among her lovers most of the dandies of *La Comédie humaine* from Rastignac to Maxime de Trailles decides that the only man who can satisfy her is a genius, d'Arthez—who usually appears as Balzac's fondest vision of himself. Realising that her past is against her, she is inspired to present herself to him as a simple and virginal character, grossly calumniated by the world. She plays this part so beautifully—and with such generosity, as it is for his sake that she wants to renew her virginity—that she convinces him. So when her dear friend Madame d'Espard invites all the former lovers to dinner with d'Arthez, to disillusion him, he smiles with unshakable confidence at their calumnies. One of them is forced to admit that genius is stronger than truth.

Diane and d'Arthez retire to enjoy their love beside an Alpine lake, which to Balzac is always the image of an idyll (*Albert Savarus*), as it was there that he first won Madame Hanska, and there that he had imagined the winning of Madame de Castries: the lakes of Bourget, Neuchâtel, and Geneva held his torments and his joys.

This *Secrets de la princesse de Cadignan*, which re-unites so many favourites of *La Comédie humaine*, has some claim to be a revelation of the whole work, for it is an extreme development of two master themes, firstly that will and feeling can triumph over the most indis-putable facts, secondly that women are not, like men, enclosed in the limits of their own egoism, but can achieve entire transformations of their natures.

As women are, at least to Balzac, the more devoted gender, the two themes become one: femine intensity presides over creation.

This drastic reassertion of feminine values explains his deep appeal to women readers in his day, for his physi-ology of women is very much deeper than his *Physiologie du mariage*, which was no more than a first youthful manifesto on their behalf. What is constant in Balzac is belief in passion for its own sake, which explains his admiration for Napoleon, who believed in power for its own sake. Balzac's claim to complete with the pen what he had begun with the sword meant the same devotion to an absolute. But because this absolute was conceived in feminine terms, it could become oddly domesticated.

Balzac believed in passion so absolutely that he hardly distinguished between the affairs of a Diane de Maufrigneuse or even those of la Torpille and the sacri-fices of an Adeline Hulot or even a Madame de la Chan-terie, for they were all giving as he gave himself to his work. He could approve the passion of Coralie or la Torpille for the handsome Lucien only less than the celestial passion of Séraphita. So passion could be domesticated in a Josephine Claes or an Adeline Hulot and not lose its force, even gain more intensity.

He was a novelist seeking to magnify life, not a moral-

ist trying to enforce a code, yet because he was giving
birth to books as a woman to children, he had a woman's
demand for faith in love. The disastrous passions which
he expressed so potently in his work, Goriot's for his
daughters, Grandet's for his money, Claes's for his
alchemy, Birotteau's for his shop, are not only distinct
from love, but wholly opposed to it. Goriot's passion
became obsessive only when the death of his wife
destroyed the peace of his love, his wife even halted
Grandet, as his Josephine was able to control Balthazar
Claes, and Madame Birotteau was always trying to check
her César's ambition. Passion in Balzac achieves its worst
disasters only when it escapes from the control of women,
for even Hulot, ruined by them, is corrupted only because
he eludes his wife and goes from bad to worse and uglier
women, driven by his own lust, not by their qualities,
nor in the end even by their charms.

The criminal passion of Vautrin himself is typified in
the remark of the detective that "he does not care for
women."

Yet even Napoleon, despite his belief in power, or because of it, imposed a code on France and came to terms
with the Church, and so Balzac, despite his belief in
passion, imposed a code and a religion on *La Comédie
humaine,* in the Preface to which he insisted that Christianity was a complete system of control over the depraved
tendencies of man, who could be restrained only by
religion: the family, not the individual, was the unit of
society.

This again is very feminine, to emphasize the importance of passionate feelings and nature, only to demand
their submission to the family and piety. Reconciliation
of the two is not impossible, though Balzac himself
showed their divergence in *Mémoires de deux jeunes
mariées.* There are interesting differences in his own
attempts at a happy solution in the two works instanced

above, *Les Secrets de la princesse de Cadignan* and
Modeste Mignon. The first is almost a fantasy, for it is
hard to believe that *la belle Diane* and the incorruptible
d'Arthez really lived happily ever afterwards—they were
at least unlikely to found a family. The happiness of
Modeste is more secure, but the dedication of her story
to Madame Hanska draws attention to the difference in
age between the literary and the real couples. *Modeste
Mignon* is a vision of what might have been, not of what
happened—unless Balzac's marriage a few months before
his death is to be seen as a happy ending.

The vitality of his women really springs from the
force with which he loves them. Each one of them came
to him, working in the night, as a vision of desire. Even
Madame Vauquer in *Goriot* becomes for a moment desir-
able on the evening when she dresses up for Vautrin,
even the fishergirl of *La Rabouilleuse* can arouse passions. That is why they are superior to his men, for there
is more of his vision in them, more of his desire, making
them subjectively richer in life.

He wanted happiness for them, as he wanted the
women he loved to be happy with him, sometimes
indulging himself with visions of union with Diane de
Maufrigneuse—in whom there is a trace of the Countess
Guidoboni-Visconti—or with Madame Hanska. But in
his love for them he put himself in their place, to perceive
that some wanted drama more than happiness in their
lives. So he put them in situations where they could
display their "enchanting" or their "sublime" qualities.
But his vision was so intense that they became more
vivid than their models in real life. Until he was already
dying, Madame Hanska preferred seeing herself in his
pages to being no more than his wife.

Women recognised themselves in his work because
his vision of them was so close to their own. That was
how they behaved—in their dreams. Only one of them,

Madame de Berny, came to him before the work was written, and by her encouragement made it possible. Only she was both a real woman and a Balzac heroine, a vision that came to him before he had acquired the power of vision. That is why she remained NUNC ET SEMPER DILECTA, loved now and for ever.

5

The Short Stories

THE TECHNIQUE of Balzac's short stories is more widely admired than that of his novels. Certainly it is very different, but it is proof of his skill as a writer that he had so sharp a sense of the difference between the two techniques. Yet one particular his short stories and his novels have in common, for both begin with the creation of an atmosphere appropriate to the theme.

Obviously in a short story there was no room for details of house, furniture, clothes, streets, or countryside which often projected the atmosphere in his novels. The effect had to be immediate, but a swift movement into action or a beginning in a drama already developed, such as is often used today, would not have suited his method which, being visual, depended so much on the setting of a scene. Instead, he chose themes that depended on their appeal to the most prompt of human emotions, such as horror and humour, to produce an impression as sudden as a shriek or a laugh.

Paul Bourget was the first to point out how Balzac also used a third means to solve the problem of the short story, by setting his scene in historical circumstances which are general knowledge, such as the Terror or the Retreat from Moscow. The use of characters already famous, such as Dante, Don Juan, or Melmoth, is another part of the same device which shortens exposition.

One result of a technique chiefly dependent on these means was to divide the short stories from the central block of *La Comédie humaine,* which is built to so much larger a design, and conceived on wholly different lines. Balzac included his short stories in it, but they had much more in common with the *Contes drolatiques.* That he was aware of this is shown by his placing most of the short stories among the *Études philosophiques,* where he put work which had no obvious relation to his map of society. The ninth volume of the Pléiade edition, the only one devoted wholly to this section, contains thirteen short stories as against only two novels. The most in any other volume are in the first, *Scènes de la vie privée,* only seven—excluding the shorter *nouvelles* which, though brief, belong more properly to *La Comédie humaine.* Nor are these genuine short stories, but short novels which form a natural sequence with the others.

Of the other short stories in the remaining volumes some, especially *La Messe de l'athée* and *Facino Cane,* might well have been placed in the philosophical section, and are best considered with that group. There are in all over twenty genuine short stories, even apart from the *Contes drolatiques,* themselves fine examples of the same art.

In his short stories, even more than in his novels, Balzac shows two of his chief qualities, his intellect and the breadth of his vision. These stories are very pointed, very definite, but the moral they point has two heads to its argument. They have their own life, but as life itself they can be taken either lightly or tragically. This appears clearly in one of the best, *Le Chef d'œuvre inconnu,* in which Porbus and the young Poussin go to see a masterpiece at which a painter of great reputation has been working for years. They know that such a work can only be extraordinary—and it is, for years of toil have created a wilderness of lines from which dimly emerges one exquisite feature. This may be regarded either as a satire on abstract art, written a century early, or as an intellectual defence of it—and it has been published with illustrations by Picasso.

In *L'Élixir de longue vie* Don Juan's father asks on his deathbed to be anointed with a liquid that will renew his life. Juan thinks the old man is delirious, but humours him, touches his eye, and finds the drug effective, whereupon he lets his father die and keeps the precious stuff for himself. When his hour comes, he knows his own pious son will not play him such a trick, but the son is so overpowered by the result that he treats only the head and arm, then collapses and drops the bottle. The awful consequence is regarded as a miracle, and the resurrected head is placed on an altar from which it blasphemes, falls, and kills the officiating priest.

This again is an equal satire on Don Juan and on the priest. It is also close to the point of *La Peau de chagrin* —the impossibility of cheating the laws of life. Similarly *Melmoth réconcilié* shows how fatal is the fulfilment of desire, a power so terrible that the possessor's only concern is to hand it on to somebody else. Balzac was constantly obsessed with the illusion of desires and the terror of their fulfilment: most of his characters are driven to a satisfaction of their passions which is also their destruction. That he worked himself to death and died when he had gained the woman of his deepest illusions are only consequences of the same law, which to him was both a law of nature and one with preternatural sanctions. So Balthazar Claes, after ruining himself and his children in pursuit of the Absolute, cries his triumphant "Eureka" on his deathbed.

The most extraordinary and the most horrible of the short stories are those in which the atmosphere and spirit of place are most carefully evoked. This is partly to balance the outrage with the reality, as in the novels the most devastating passions receive the most detailed background, but it is also because certain places breed their own dramas, and awareness of this in the reader enables the writer to save space. So Balzac has only to introduce Corsicans, and the tragedy of *La Vendetta* becomes acceptable. So the most horrible of the stories, *El Verdugo*, the Executioner, could happen only in Spain: in this the Spanish father begs that his son should be spared to continue the family which has been condemned for insurrection against the French invaders. The French general grants the request on condition that the son himself act as executioner to the rest of the family, including his own mother and sisters, who implore him to accept. He agrees—though one of his sisters is sad to think how lonely he will be without them—a character-istically "sublime" Balzac touch, here more convincing because the land is Spain, with its own attitude to death.

This unity of mood and land is preserved in other stories. *Massimila Doni* has exactly the corruption, the passion, and the music appropriate to Venice. *Facino Cane*, who is also a Venetian, has its secrecy and its wealth. So *Sarrasine* and *Gambara* have their Romans and Italians, always held up by Balzac as by Stendhal to be examples of sincerity and devotion to art. So Thaddée Paç's fantasy and chivalry in *La Fausse maîtresse* are more readily grasped because he is a Pole. So *Un Drame au bord de la mer* owes something of its horror to the bleak salt marshes of southern Brittany.

In some stories the background of the Terror itself provides the suspense. In *Le Réquisitionnaire* a mother prepares a room for her royalist son which is requisitioned for the agent sent to arrest him. That is a more obvious effect than *Un Épisode sous la Terreur* where the execu-tioner has a mass said for the king he has executed—an act paralleled by the atheist doctor in *La Messe d'un athée* who against all his convictions has a mass said for the old porter who had helped him in his student days, knowing that it is what would most have pleased him.

Balzac was often attracted by a particular sort of incongruity, behavior out of character that has a fantastic explanation, either owing to a peculiar incident in the past or to pressure of circumstance. He was always looking for the revealing circumstance or the telling moment, as he describes himself at the beginning of *Facino Cane:*

> With me observation had become intuitive; it did not neglect the body, but it penetrated further, into the soul or rather it grasped the outer details so completely that it at once passed beyond them. It gave me the ability to live the life of another, substituting myself for him. . . .

It was in fact because he walked in this dream of creation that he saw details and breathed in atmosphere with such intensity, for they were absorbed unconsciously and returned to him afterwards charged with all the force of his vision: as a man remembers years afterwards every detail of a room where he received some great shock, even when the memory of the shock itself has faded. This is the meaning of his remark that he never had time to observe, for what appears in his work as detailed observation was really a memory, chiefly of those desperate and haunted years between twenty and thirty, when he still could neither make nor sign his name. This is why his works, for all their detail, have the obsessive reality of a dream, and the fact that he often worked in a state of exhaustion in the hours before the dawn made him more dependent on the phantoms in the back of his mind. At such a time and in such a condition, the mind is least rational and most open to strange interpretations. His emphasis on the preternatural and the extraordinary in his short stories, some of which were written at a sitting, owe something to this circumstance.

M. Albert Béguin says that the short stories are all written by Louis Lambert—that is, that Balzac's intellectual nature and his preoccupation with the other world are most evident in them. Certainly they are more nakedly revealed there, especially in such a story as *Les Proscrits,* where Dante listens in Paris to a lecture by Siger of Brabant and hears remarks on the angels and celestial truths which might well have issued from Louis Lambert.

What is not often emphasized is that there was in Balzac something of a real scholar, eccentric and undisciplined, but with that gift of extra perception which is sometimes accorded to the amateur. Such a work as *Sur Catherine de Médicis* shows a real insight into the history of the sixteenth century. But his historical genius is nowhere more obvious than in the *Contes drolatiques,* which are even written in sixteenth century French.

It is not for a foreigner to estimate the accuracy with which this language is reproduced—it has been criticized —but it is at the least an astonishing pastiche. The stories themselves are very much more than that, for they have an authentic savour of the period, that gaiety of the Renaissance in which still grinned the gargoyles of the Middle Ages.

They are of course directly inspired by Rabelais, and offered to him as a tribute from another son of Touraine, but the subjects owe considerably more to the *fabliaux* long before him. Some critics of Balzac, like some of his women correspondents, have tended to devote all their attention to *La Comédie humaine* and to dismiss the *Contes drolatiques* as a lapse of taste in a genius not easy to pardon. This has made the difference between the man and the work even harder to explain, for the

Contes drolatiques are a most valuable aid to the understanding of Balzac.

First, it is hard to emphasize enough the directness of
his descent from Rabelais, on which he himself insisted
so much, not only in these stories, but in the original
preface to *La Peau de chagrin*. Like Rabelais, he had an
exuberance of temperament which could suddenly
quieten into good sense. Like Rabelais, he had a passion
for learning and for science which could issue into startling applications. Like Rabelais, he had a deep respect
for the heritage and traditions of the past combined
with impatience and contempt for their orthodox de-
fenders and for received opinions. Then while Rabelais
was also a doctor who dissected the human body, Balzac
was also a sociologist who dissected the body politic.
If Rabelais was much more of a satirist, his attacks on
the Sorbonne can be paralleled by Balzac's on the journalists and publicists of his day.

Second, the *Contes drolatiques* and this affinity with
Rabelais reveal how much Balzac was really a man of
the Renaissance. Victor Hugo's aims and ideals were
typical of the nineteenth century which accorded him so
much honour, and his interest in the past was romantic,
antiquarian, picturesque, but Balzac really preferred the
sixteenth century—and immensely preferred Catherine de
Médicis to Louis-Philippe. Whenever he mentions the
sixteenth century it is with enthusiasm, not only for its
art, but even for its politics. He was a man of the
Renaissance in the fantasy and eccentricity of his scientific interests, in fixing his eyes on an ideal Woman
while having affairs with women of flesh and blood, in
his odd theological speculations and his championship of
the Church. Even what is often considered a typical
foible of his own—his exaggerated deference for the great
and his no less exalted sense of the respect due to artists
—becomes more understandable when referred to some

of Vasari's stories about Michelangelo, Leonardo, or
Raphael—Raphael, whose tastes were almost more luxurious than Balzac's, and who was even more notorious for
his affairs with women.

If some have been puzzled by a certain grossness in
Balzac, going with a great delicacy of feeling and deep
intellectual preoccupations, this was much more common
in the Renaissance, and Balzac's speculations were less
startling than those of Pico de Mirandola, as his lavishness
was less than Raphael's. So too his interest in the pre-
ternatural and in fortunetelling or prophecies was more
usual in the age of Nostradamus.

It might even be maintained that the *Contes drolatiques* represent the fundamental Balzac, who supplied the
energy and insight which went to the greater achievement
of *La Comédie humaine*. On this thesis he would be a
great comic writer turned by the Revolution's effect on
France, the grim aftermath of its wars, the temper of the
time, and the vogue of the novel into one more tragic—
which would at least explain the contrast between the
joyous vitality of his writing and the grimness of his
material. But the point has not to be pressed so far,
because in fact there is much in common between *La
Comédie humaine* and the *Contes drolatiques,* which
have themselves grimness interleaved with their humour.

The reason why they appear so authentic, so much in
the spirit of an earlier age, is that Balzac almost
wholly lacked a quality often valued by critics today
under the name of "compassion," which arises from a
moral judgment or a protest on the conditions of human
existence. Most generations select some quality to value
as peculiarly their own—Balzac was similarly addicted to
the "sublime," but he had none of this "compassion," as
he wrote in a tradition that reasoned less about the work-
ings of fate, with the result that tragedies and comedies
were less sharply distinguished.

This is most striking in the *Contes drolatiques*, that tragedies and comedies not only jostle each other in these stories, but even occur in the same story, which gives both a vivid impression of an age in which gaiety and sudden death were close companions, and emphasizes a fact not always noted by writers—that in real life grief itself is never safe from the touch of farce, nor is any delight secure from the jab of pain.

Art, however emancipated or abstract, has to limit itself to a form and a style, if only because pictures, buildings, books, are restricted by size, place, circumstance, while life is free to be more incongruous. In the *Contes drolatiques* Balzac comes near to this sort of freedom because he uses the grotesque to confront kings, village girls, and monks in an incongruity which is not forced, but has the casual quality of real life.

These stories have often been regarded as a thing apart in his work, but once disengaged from their archaic language and sixteenth century background, figures and situations disclose resemblances with those in *La Comédie humaine*.

There is even, strangest case of all in this collection of "gay science," one story, *Le Frère d'armes*, which has something in it of *Séraphita* and the sublime, as it ends:

> The lady broke into tears, admiring this noble fidelity, this sublime resignation in his faith, and the exalted sufferings of this inner passion. But as she too had preserved her love in the depths of her heart she died when Lavalière perished before the gates of Metz.

La Connétable is as nobly served by her lover as is *La Femme de trente ans* by the devoted Arthur Grenville. *Berthe la repentie* is not unworthy of a place beside Véronique Graslin in *Le Curé de village*. The woman who is la Mye du roi has much in common with those in *Splendeurs et misères des courtisanes*, and treats her

husband with as high a hand as Esther serves the Baron
de Nucingen. Most striking case of all, la belle Impéria,
almost the hostess of the Council of Constance—and of
the *Contes drolatiques,* the first and last stories being
both dedicated to her—has much in common with the
Duchesse de Maufrigneuse, la belle Diane, who makes
ten different appearances in *La Comédie humaine.* Both
are almost fairy-tale characters for whom Balzac sus-
pends the ordinary laws of retribution, and la belle
Impéria ends by finding true love with her Isle-Adam
as la belle Diane with Daniel d'Arthez.

Le Succube, the longest of the stories in the *Contes
drolatiques,* is a masterly piece apart from the others,
also different in being set back in the Middle Ages, not
in the Renaissance, but it has as remarkable a sense
of period. In it a Saracen girl enters a convent, but returns
into the world where she entrances so many lovers that
she acquires power and wealth which she uses gener-
ously for the poor and for the Church, but an ambitious
cleric brings a case against her as an enchantress, causing
riots in Tours, and she is burned. The story is told in
extracts from thirteenth century archives of the cathedral,
concluding with a later document that proves her
innocence.

As *La Peau de chagrin* uses the device of a magic skin
to represent the mortal skin of a man's life, equal in their
brevity, so *Le Succube* uses a girl's genuine charms to
credit her with the reputation of an enchantress. The
skill of both narratives lies in the exact balance between
the natural and the supernatural—they can be taken either
way, because the results remain the same, whatever the
causes. *Le Succube* through her own arts can give her
clerical rider the illusion of being transported to heaven,
as her diabolical arts can show him the generation of
worlds in the seeds of the Milky Way. A vision remains a
vision, in the real world or in the imagination.

Because they reveal so clearly Balzac's sense of the equality between reality and vision—to him interchangeable—the *Contes drolatiques* illuminate *La Comédie humaine*, which is a vision of nineteenth century France, parallel to theirs of sixteenth century Touraine. The times had changed, but the fantasy remains the same, for Balzac's women and men chase similar dreams in the sunshine of comedy or in the darkness of tragedy. But in *La Comédie humaine* they are pretending to be grown-up, while in the *Contes drolatiques* they are content to remain the children of his fantasy.

Genius and Passion

IF, TO SOME, Vautrin appears the most powerful figure in Balzac's work, it is not only because he so dominates both his fellow criminals and those in other fictions, nor even because he can remain so much himself under the most fantastic disguises, but because he represents so strongly a basic element in *La Comédie humaine* and in Balzac himself.

Both Vautrin and Balzac seek to impose themselves on a society in which there is no place for them, and to achieve this they have only their intelligence and their personality—no influence beyond that, no helpful relations in the world, no money, no established position. Both have to make a career for themselves, and this is true of many others in *La Comédie humaine,* for even those in better positions are trying to impose themselves on either women or society, while many of the women are making similar efforts to conquer a man or a social stronghold. But the struggles of Vautrin the criminal and Balzac the writer are peculiarly intense because they face special difficulties.

Every artist is a criminal in that he has to upset established values to make a place for himself in society which already has its own pictures and books and possessions, and it naturally defends them against attack from criminals and artists and writers, who compel the making of fresh purchases and judgments to replace those which have been stolen or devalued.

When an artist has achieved a position or a writer has "made his name," he is no less concerned to defend it than a thief who has reformed or retired, yet Balzac not only remembered his struggles but continued them, for he was always attempting a greater work, and indeed died before he had completed his own plan for *La Comédie humaine*, which was to have contained one hundred and thirty-seven titles as against the ninety-one which he completed.

For this reason his conservative opinions were modified by his active sympathy with ambition and by his own, as he was also disillusioned not only by conservative politicians but by most established figures in a society which in his view they were corrupting more than they were supporting: in his work an honest banker or businessman is even rarer than an honest lawyer—Birotteau and Derville are both noted as exceptions in their integrity.

So while he accepted the institutions of that society, he remained bitterly opposed to all those, whether men of affairs or ministers, who corrupted the country by graft and theft committed inside the law. In *La Maison Nucingen* in which he exposed some of the financial tricks of the day, he noted that a clever and unscrupulous man could ruin thousands, yet acquire the title of baron and an honoured position in society, while one who had purloined food for his hungry family went to prison. A government could default on a loan with disastrous effects on wide areas, yet remain in power, while an honest man could be driven to bankruptcy and ruin. At the time, the development of large capital had been so swift that safeguards had not yet been enforced, and banking was considerably in advance of insurance.

People were protesting against the absolute power of kings or the ambitions of generals when this power had already passed into the hands of financiers.

Some of Balzac's own ventures, in printing, in publishing, in journalism, had been frustrated by the wiles of lawyers and moneylenders, and he had a bitter experience of their trickery. When he saw their legalised theft of property he had more sympathy for the crimes of a Vautrin, who at least had more courage and less hypocrisy—and what appealed most to Balzac—an audacity and lightheartedness similar to those of more Bohemian artists.

That he remained well able to distinguish between a principle and its abuse, Balzac showed in his introduction to *L'Élixir de longue vie,* where he gives a horrifying account of those who wait eagerly for the death of relations from whom they are going to inherit. Some, like Don Juan in this story, not only do all they can to hasten the end of their parents, but even bring it about. Yet, says Balzac, this is no valid argument against inheritance, on which all civilisation is based.

At the same time, pressed for money as he often was and having the expensive tastes that sometimes drive to crime, he preferred the frank criminal to the hypocrite who may commit worse crimes without endangering either his safety or his reputation. When Vautrin in *Goriot* speaks of ambitious men who are above the ordinary conventions of human conduct, Balzac had little difficulty in finding words to justify him, and Rastignac after his first insight into the corruption of Paris society has to admit that Vautrin is no worse—and much more honest. Balzac himself, in adhering to the legitimist party and shocking those who were most devoted to him, Madame de Berny and Zulma Carraud, had known that ambition could corrupt, for he shared with Vautrin and Rastignac their passion for money, luxury, and power.

When the crisis came, Rastignac drew back from conniving at murder, and Vautrin had to drug him to prevent his going to the police. So Balzac, drugged by his hopes of Madame de Castries and a political future, failed for an interval to champion the forces of law and order against Vautrin, but his clarity of mind quickly recovered, as he had a stronger head than a Lucien who wholly succumbed to the domination of Vautrin. *Goriot* may be a greater work than *Splendeurs et misères des courtisanes* which completes the Vautrin cycle, but the abbé Herrera is a more impressive image of Vautrin, who is most convincing of all in his "last incarnation"—when he shows his complete mastery over all other criminals in the prison yard, and then places his gifts at the disposal of the authorities.

In this, Vautrin was a true figure of Balzac himself, who attacked the society of his day with such vehemence, and ended by becoming a part of it, so that his work retains the traits of Louis-Philippe's reign, though he so much despised him. But this was not simply a development of Balzac's thought, which was conservative even before he first wrote of Vautrin, who was more the means by which he expressed his disgust and horror with the corruption and injustice of a society which he still preferred to the anarchy and cruelty of revolutions.

It has often enough been remarked that Balzac's characters have the energy of his genius, or as Baudelaire said, they are all bursting with determination. But there is a sense in which all the obsessed characters, Vautrin, Goriot, Grandet, Claes, the chasers of an absolute in power, feeling, wealth, or knowledge, are morally lesser and weaker men then himself, because they were dominated by passions which they were unable to control, while he was able to check their effects in his own life precisely because he expressed them sufficiently in his work.

Vautrin here, though less pathetic and less moving than
Goriot, has a greater interest for that work as a whole,
because he is the incarnation of absolute power, the
Napoleon of *La Comédie humaine*, and Balzac's attitude
to him is as ambivalent as it was to Napoleon himself.

Balzac was constantly exercised by the tension between
human determination and destiny. This to him was even
the basic problem of religion, for Louis Lambert found
the inequality of human destiny the greatest obstacle to
his belief in God. The power of his genius led Balzac to
belief that only the greatest energy and determination,
his own or a Napoleon's, could effect any enduring work
in the world. In this struggle he was tempted to believe
in power for its own sake, and in money as the chief
instrument of power. If only he had enough money, he
would be free to produce works of genius, as when he
had achieved power, Napoleon had created an empire
for France. "Destiny is politics," had been Napoleon's
dismissal of the problem. Balzac, in his sphere, was
tempted to think that destiny was money.

Yet Napoleon's determination had brought him to his
destiny at Waterloo and St. Helena. Balzac, meditating
the lesson, had seen that Goriot's determination to safe-
guard his daughters had brought him to delirium and
death, while Claes's had ruined his family.

Vautrin's case is one more profound and more useful
to Balzac, as his ambition is less simple, for although he
wants to retire to his plantation with hundreds of slaves,
and needs money for this, he already has enough to
achieve one great satisfaction, power over men. His
personality is such that his fellow criminals have already
placed their funds with him, and use him as their banker.
His intelligence and his disguises enable him to assume
a part, even that of a priest, and play it to such perfection
that he makes converts, as he saves Lucien from suicide
to endow him with a million and engage him to a duke's

daughter. Yet Lucien commits suicide in the end, and
Vautrin too is frustrated in his ambition.

Vautrin's ambition, like Balzac's, was obscure even to
himself. He was seduced by dreams of opulence and
leisure, yet he was happiest in manipulating the lives of
others, in planning brilliant futures for a Rastignac or a
Lucien. So Balzac was happiest in controlling the lives of
his characters, in the power with which he found positions in the government for a Marsay or a Rastignac,
happiness in marriage for an Ursule or a Modeste. Yet
these successes, like Vautrin's, were combined with the
bankruptcy of a Birotteau, the tragedy of a Goriot, the
disappointments of a Madame de Beauséant or a Comtesse d'Aiglemont. He could give to his characters his
own determination, as Vautrin could bend Lucien to his
will, but they were still unable to escape the power of
destiny.

Balzac was constantly learning from his characters
the fatal nature of his own passions. If in *La Peau de
chagrin* he had a first prophetic vision of his own life,
in other novels he discovered the frustration of its
different phases. His anxiety over money and the debts
he had contracted in his twenties, which weighed on him
all his life, weighed too on all his characters. Their preoccupation with rents and incomes, calculated to the
last franc, drove them to dreams of fortune, rich mar-
riages, inheritance, even, as in the case of Vautrin, to
crime. Their dreams were also his own, and he tried to
shake them off in his writing, but always the debts kept
ahead even of his labours.

In his own case, some of his money troubles were
caused by simple material obstacles, such as his fantastic
methods of composition—he sent even his briefest drafts
to the printer, had them set with excessively wide mar-
gins, wrote most of the book in galley, demanding more
and more proofs. These proofs are hardly credible to

those who have not seen them (a mass of erasures, additions, bubbles, lines, deletions, corrections), and they were hardly legible to the printer who refused to do more than "a page of Balzac" at a time: the strain was too great.

Yet even this was only a symptom of his wider extravagance, his dress, his carriages, his houses, especially the disastrous building of Les Jardies, then the final phase of bric-à-bracomania, when he was acquiring pictures, furniture, vases, and tapestries for the Pavillon Beaujon in anticipation of his marriage to Madame Hanska.

So the debts and the pressure of creditors continued, while the cost of printing his books diminished the profits of publishing them. He worked harder and harder, both to correct and improve his writing and to earn, to pay his way, to live. But the conscience of the writer and the anxiety of the man were in conflict, and the need for money to free him from the harshness of his destiny became an obsession which was transferred to all his characters, for whom he worked out elaborate columns of profit and loss, with exact details, as he had so often stared at such figures himself. They conducted a vendetta against him hardly less implacable than those figures of his *Histoire des treize* who so persecuted the young baron in *Ferragus*. When he was engaged in his struggle with Buloz who closed much of the Paris press to him, forcing him to start his own journal and so incur more debts, he had reason to feel that he was being hunted like a criminal.

Yet in his efforts to baffle his creditors, while labouring to pay his debts, Balzac more often appeared as a comic figure, though the man whom he had acknowledged as his first master, Walter Scott, has always been respected as a noble figure in his work on the Waverley novels, similarly undertaken to honour his engagements. Balzac should at least receive the honour which is due to such efforts, as described in *La Grandeur et décadence de César Birotteau*, for he had been tricked as Birotteau had been when he was first saddled with debt, even if he also shared Birotteau's ambition and expansive hopes.

The financial details which so accumulate in *La Comédie humaine* are commonly ascribed to Balzac's realism, but they owe more to his anxieties and an imagination constantly haunted by debt and by fantastic schemes to acquire the wealth which alone could relieve him. The two things fused in his mind as in those of all harassed and dreaming of first prize in a sweepstake or lottery—a large part of humanity, in fact. Because the part is so large, because it is the fate of man constantly to dream of an easier life, Balzac's own dreams appeared as realism in his description of French society, but this was only because in all his visions this was the point at which he was closest to a common interest.

His first illusions of success in publishing and printing, his fantastic journey to Sardinia in 1837 in search of the old Roman silver mines, his certainties of a fortune from growing pineapples at Les Jardies, transporting them to Paris by the new railway, and even at Wierzchownia his plan to export timber to France for railway sleepers, all these illusions, some of which prospered in the hands of others more fortunate or less extravagant than himself, stimulated his dreams of fortune attained.

They were available for *La Comédie humaine* where they were transferred into figures and accounts accurate enough in themselves, but both in origin and in development not the most realistic but the most fantastic part of his work.

Yet if he had experience of illusions he had even more of their frustration and disappointment, which also found their place in his work. In this interplay of illusion and disappointment he uncovered the answer to the basic problem of life, which had perplexed Louis Lambert, which had been posed in *La Peau de chagrin:* is real satisfaction and the meaning of life to be found in desire and the determination to achieve it, or are the circumstances of a man's life beyond his control, what is often called destiny, his only happiness a recognition of this?

The answer that Balzac gave in his work closely accorded with Napoleon's "destiny is politics," for in its simplest form it becomes "destiny is character," as a man's character is shaped by his passions, the paternal passion of a Goriot, the avarice of a Grandet, the criminal passion of a Vautrin, the celestial passion of a Séraphita: all are responsible for the course their lives assume, their destinies, whether as a father, a miser, a criminal, or an angel.

So simply stated, the answer is obvious, but it involves another truth less widely accepted, the truth of *La Peau de chagrin,* that all desires are self-destructive, that all destinies are in the end frustrated, not only because men die, but because desires themselves die, even before death, and they die most swiftly of all when they are most completely satisfied.

The extraordinary element in Balzac's life is that, while he discovered this truth so clearly in his work, he never applied it to himself. Goriot has no wish to be anything but Goriot, the devoted father of his daughters, but Balzac was constantly trying not to be Balzac, the prolific author of *La Comédie humaine,* the devoted father of so many characters.

If he had achieved any of his dearest desires, whether as a political leader, the proprietor of a silver mine, or even as the husband of a rich wife, he would have abandoned those labours on which his destiny depended. In fact, the nearer he came to marriage with Madame Hanska, the less he wrote. It was true that he had moments of exuberance in which he spoke of his work as a vast cathedral, but if the ultimate pressure was his own genius, the immediate urge was the hard necessity of his circumstances.

His desires too were self-destructive, for when they were fulfilled he was no longer the living writer of genius but the dying husband of Madame Hanska. Yet even in his own life he uncovered the deeper truth of his work, for he too was driven to his destiny by his passions and desires. What he had failed to understand, in common with his characters, was that the obstacles in his way, the debts, the checks to his career, the breakdown of his financial projects, the delay in marriage to Madame Hanska, or even the earlier fiasco of Les Jardies, were not really obstacles but stimulants to his work.

So Goriot failed to realise that he was spoiling his daughters, Claes that he was ruining his family. They felt that they were being frustrated by what were really the consequences of their own passions. So Balzac brought disaster on his finances and ruined his health, feeling that he was being frustrated by circumstances beyond his control, when the passion of his own genius was responsible, for it was only in his work that he was really himself.

In this unconsciousness of reality Balzac was wonderfully faithful to the principles of his characters, as it is a necessary condition of passion and desire that they should work in ignorance. The more obsessed a man is, the more he feels that his obsession is a necessary condition of life: Grandet believes that the hoarding of money is obvious common sense, Goriot that his father's feelings are the most natural in the world, Claes that nothing is so important as the transmutation of metals which is the discovery of the Absolute. They are not mad, for they recognize the existence of other motives. Grandet finds it extraordinary that his daughter Eugénie should spend money, Claes that Josephine or Margurite should not accept the ruin of the family's fortunes when they would be immensely enriched by the discovery of the Absolute.

Sometimes, even in literary matters where he was usually more serious, Balzac was no less contemptuous of reality. Gautier relates an extraordinary episode when Balzac summoned him to help write a play which was to be shown to a producer the next day. Balzac would write three of the acts, Gautier two. But when Gautier not unreasonably asked what the plot was to be, Balzac was indignant: "We can't stop to discuss that or we'll never finish in time." Claes himself could not have been more impatient at an interruption to his chemical experiments. So Balzac was impatient of realities outside his work, as when he said to Sandeau, who was talking of his father's serious condition, "That's all very well, but let's return to reality. Who is going to marry Eugénie Grandet?"

As art was stronger than life in him, for his work killed him when he was just over fifty, so his vision was stronger than reality. In fact, vision to him was reality, as the "return to reality" was simply to his vision of the Grandets at Saumur.

It is here that the figure of Vautrin acquires its full meaning, for he is at once the most fantastic character in *La Comédie humaine* and one most closely drawn from real life, or so Balzac himself claimed. It is known that Vautrin was largely based on Vidocq who similarly established himself as a leader among criminals, then offered his services to the police whom he served until he relapsed with the accomplishment of a particularly well conceived crime. This last detail was not copied, for the Vautrin cycle ends with his admission into the police, but Balzac also drew on the experience of other criminals, one of whom he closely questioned at Les Jardies. He was in fact very careful of accuracy in character, in clothing, in furniture, in houses, in streets, in towns.

But, as with Vautrin, the closer he comes to reality, the greater is the stimulus to his fantasy.

He established himself inside a character very much as he set himself up in a house or apartment, one outwardly very suitably placed in a Paris street, even if it had some peculiarity, a concealed door at the side or, in grander days in the rue Fortunée, one leading into a church, but inside it was furnished with his own fantasy, whether it was the bare garret recalled in *Facino Cane* or the luxurious apartment described in *La Fille aux yeux d'or*. Anyhow, once inside the character or the house, he remained implacably Balzac, with his monkish robe and his coffee maker, above all with his vision and his fantasy.

The elements supplied by a Vidocq were as exact and solid as the masonry, but inside them Balzac was free to develop all the vagaries of his own character. Vautrin ceases to be Vidocq, because he becomes Balzac, who had early claimed the gift of being able to transfer himself into the skin of another person, like a djinn in the Arabian Nights. That is why *La Comédie humaine*, for all the exactitude of its detail and all its historical value, has the charm of a fairyland, even and perhaps most of all in its horrors, as there are worse butcheries in the Arabian Nights, more horrors in the fairy tales of the brothers Grimm. There is even something childlike in a writer who can describe such matters almost with relish.

But Balzac needed the traits and streets of other people before he could release his vision, as he needed a house in which to write. It was only when he had adopted the mask of Vautrin that he could express all his very real contempt for a society in which some men were honoured for their adventures and intelligence in accumulating wealth, while others were condemned for escapades which sprang from a character more violent but in some particulars less morally corrupt. It was only by speaking as an antisocial criminal that he could uncover the worst corruptions, as it was only by speaking as Benassis, the country doctor, that he could defend the health of a properly constituted society.

In this, some of Vautrin's tirades or the lectures of Benassis to Genestas come close to the dramatic monologues of Browning, who equally adopted masks that were not his own to express the views of a Blougram or a Sludge.

Balzac was in fact more a poet than a philosopher, and the historical value of his work is a product of his vision, as historical facts are also to be found in primitive epics. He was describing not only a more complex society, but one which was rapidly changing under his eyes. His own restlessness and the vicissitudes of his brief life enabled him to interpret these changes not simply as an observer but as an actor. He could rise to ministerial rank with a Rastignac, endure the miseries of Paris journalism with a Rubempré, hoard the secrets of society with a Gobseck, and most intimately of all feel power over those he manipulated with Vautrin, unrestrained by any code or convention.

There is in all *La Comédie humaine* something of Vautrin's power, genial yet contemptuous not only of laws but even of life, as Vautrin cynically had Taillefer's son killed or more abominably drove Peyrade's daughter out of her mind. So Balzac, unlike Dickens ("indulgent father to the children of his fancy") killed off the brilliant Louis Lambert, or more brutally allowed the innocent Pierette to die under persecution, if that was necessary to his plans.

He was so much inside Vautrin that he had to distinguish himself from him, and he remarked the difference by emphasizing one side of Vautrin's character—"he was not interested in women." Nobody could say that of Balzac. He could have found no more telling point by which to underline not only his difference from Vautrin but from the theory of male egoism and power which he embodied. For ultimately the whole of Balzac's work and the society he described rest not on the aggressive passions of men, but on the women whose sacrifices and devotion assured its survival.

Society and Piety

THE BALZAC who has been most prized by historians critical of the Revolution such as Taine, or by royalists such as Bainville and Gaxotte, is also the Balzac valued by Marx and Engels, or by such a follower of theirs as Professor Lukács. This is the Balzac who not only claimed to be the secretary of French society, but even asserted that it was "not enough to be a man—one has also to be a system." Yet this statement, which might well have come from the Marxist, was made by a royalist, even a legitimist.

This is already a sufficient contrast, sometimes explained by the exactitude and realism of his social analysis which has allowed both sides to find some support in his work for their own views. Yet even here, in the most systematic side of his work, Balzac had a strongly personal outlook, as is clear from his treatment of Napoleon, a figure equally uncongenial to royalists and to Marxists. For what fascinated Balzac in Napoleon was largely the quality of Vautrin, his power over men, the force of his character.

Believing that the first duty of a government was to be strong, Balzac supported firm rule whether by a king or by a republic. He pointed out that the absolute rule of Catherine II had strengthened Russia, while the weakness

of the amiable Louis XVI had destroyed the monarchy
and delivered France to the Terror. After the Revolution
of 1848 when he submitted his name for the Assembly,
Balzac declared that his first wish was that the republic
should be strong, because what France most needed was
a permanent regime, not one that changed every fifteen
years—though Heine, who had talked with him at this
time, ironically commented that what he really wanted
was a republic ruled by royalists.

The point may be taken, for there was in fact an
ambiguity in Balzac's attitude to politics, as in his attitude
to Vautrin, partly because a belief in power is itself
ambiguous, as it can be exercised for good or evil. Just
the same uncertainty extends to Napoleon: whether he
was "the heir of the Revolution" or the restorer of order
and authority.

When Victor Hugo, in his funeral oration over Balzac,
called this royalist a revolutionary writer (much to the
disgust of his widow), he was historically right in that
both Napoleon and Balzac had issued from the Revolution. They had more than that in common. Both their
families had their origins much farther south, the Bona-
partes in Corsica, the Balzacs in Gascony, and both had
come to seek power in Paris. Both were parvenus who
made terms with existing society, but they were critical
of what they found in Paris. Napoleon was not more
abrupt with political parties than Balzac with literary
groups. Both resolved to impose their own ideas, while
Napoleon's Concordat with the Church was an image
of Balzac's own accord with her place in society. Finally
both died prematurely, one at fifty-two, the other at fifty-
one.

Yet Balzac's political outlook was not Napoleon's
because a generation came between them—Balzac had
himself only just come of age when Napoleon died in
St. Helena—and France had endured other changes.

Louis XVIII, himself a shrewd politician (as shown in *Le Lys dans la vallée*) had been frustrated by the zeal of his followers and the obstinacy of his brother who, as Charles X, lost the throne in 1830 to the Orleanist branch in the person of Louis-Philippe, who changed his style from king of France to king of the French—a gesture typical of a reign of compromises inexpertly executed, the opposite of all that Balzac approved.

The effect of these changes on a supporter of stable government was to make him a legitimist, as the disorders of the Revolution had earlier been used to justify the rule of Napoleon, for Balzac believed that only a return to an undisputed succession could prevent further changes of dynasty or falls of government. It was in fact his dubious claim to the throne that brought Louis-Philippe to the uncertainties and expedients that further weakened his hold on the country. He tried first to set up a constitutional monarchy on the English model, and created barons in the same style. The prosperous bourgeois in *La Comédie humaine* all seek to become barons of this sort, such as the Baron de Nucingen, the financier whose cunning led to the comment in *La Maison Nucingen* that "highway murders were acts of charity compared with some financial combines." Journals were bought and sold, journalists forced to change their opinions from day to day, resulting in the cynicism and jobbery described in *Illusions perdues*.

The reign of Louis-Philippe from 1830 to 1848 was in fact a time of lost illusions. It was also Balzac's great productive period, only *Les Chouans* and *Physiologie du mariage* appearing before it, nothing after it. These limits are so close that it is only natural that, as almost the whole of his work appeared in the reign of Louis-Philippe, the political opinions of Balzac and his characters should refer directly to it.

A cynicism in many and a devout legitimacy in others

reflected on Louis-Philippe himself, whose father had early rallied to the Revolution, and voted for the execution of his cousin Louis XVI, only to lose his own head to the guillotine. The son of such a man, who attempted compromises of the same sort, had little to commend him to revolutionaries, who despised him both as a king and as a traitor to the Revolution, or to royalists who regarded him as the son of a regicide and a parricide.

These crosscurrents flowed through *La Comédie humaine* as in *Le Cabinet des antiques* where the old M. d'Esgrignon takes his stand on loyalty to the past, like some great tree, says Balzac, defying the force of the current, while his steward is no less commended for trying to divert that current to the benefit of his master's property.

The old d'Esgrignon remains convinced that all usurpers will perish, as Providence had disposed of Napoleon Bonaparte. Yet it is not only the old aristocracy who remain attached to the legitimist principle, which is as firmly held by the most distinguished writer, d'Arthez, who represents Balzac's finest image of himself. But the d'Arthez circle also includes the brilliant Michel Chrestien, the noble revolutionary who died on the barricades. In Balzac's world the chief opposition was not between legitimists and revolutionaries but between men of principle and the careerists—who were most typical of Louis-Philippe's reign, as the government rested on no sure principle, and ambition was the chief quality of ministers.

Balzac sympathized with ambition, as he showed in his treatment of the young Rastignac, a southerner showing some traits of Thiers, who had been born in Marseille and who attained office under Louis-Philippe. Yet Rastignac, once a minister, is no longer the attractive figure of *Goriot*, while de Marsay, who attains even higher rank, is a complete cynic, disillusioned by his first love affair,

since when he has believed "neither in God, nor man."
Yet he was a successful statesman, for he inherited from
his father, Lord Dudley, that "opportunism which is
native to the English Cabinet."

Against these careerists, Balzac asserted the principle
of legitimacy, especially in his women characters where
it almost appears as a woman's virtue, and Diane de
Maufrigneuse in composing the myth of her chastity for
d'Arthez can insist on her legitimist opinions as proof
of it. Legitimacy in this world had in fact quite the
respectability of legitimate birth.

Yet Balzac himself, in his championship of legitimacy
under the influence of Madame de Castries, was accused
even by his friends of behaving as a careerist himself.
But it was more the desire to conquer her than to conquer
Paris, where he had already triumphed, that led him to
work for the legitimist party, as the principle had for him
all the charm which la belle Diane had for d'Arthez.
When he spoke of "the purest legitimacy" it was a
feminine purity that really seduced him, as against all
the shabbiness and corruption of the regime. There was
an aesthetic element in his political opinions, as in all
his thought, for he found it difficult to give his mind to
anything that could not be transformed into the "sublime"—though this "sublimity" could appear in the dingy
deathbed of Goriot, in a Breton hut, or in a stable in the
Dauphiné.

He was disillusioned by the legitimist party, by
Madame de Castries, and by their intrigues with Paris
journalism, but when in this disillusion he attempted his
greatest political statement, *Le Médecin de campagne*,
a book much dearer to his heart than to his readers', he
was still dominated by this vision. Above all, he was
again so inspired by the Napoleonic legend that he
inserted in the book, at some loss to unity, one of its
outstanding documents, *Le Napoléon du peuple*.

It was inevitable that Balzac and his world should be
haunted by Napoleonic figures, as he was himself at the
impressionable age of sixteen when the First Empire fell,
and the Second Empire, which was based on the legend
to which he contributed, was set up two years after his
death. If he wrote during the reign of Louis-Philippe,
many of the important events in the lives of his characters had happened before then, and could only be
described by reference to Napoleon and the First Empire
—Goriot himself, the Hulots, Montriveau, and many
others, even apart from such obviously Napoleonic sur-
vivals as Colonel Chabert or Philippe Bridau in *La
Rabouilleuse*, all had their lives shaped by the Emperor.

Balzac had learned from the Duchesse d'Abrantès, the
widow of General Junot, and his wisest friend, Zulma
Carraud, was the wife of a Bonapartist officer. More important still, the Balzacs themselves owed their position
to the father's work as commissioner for the army, work
in which both Goriot and Hulot followed him. It was
perhaps with this family precedent in mind that Balzac
dedicated *Le Médecin de campagne* to his mother, his
father having died four years before. It was a book for
which he had a special regard as embodying the principles on which his work was based.

In choosing a country doctor to be spokesman of his
views, he staked his claim, advanced in the preface to
La Cousine Bette, to be "a simple doctor of social
medicine, a surgeon of incurable diseases." Benassis is
a doctor beloved by all the peasants he attends in the
mountain villages, but he is also a brilliant and dedicated
man who has renounced ambition after a tragic affair:
"For broken hearts silence among the shadows," is the
epigraph. Those of Balzac's men and women who devote
themselves to great or good works have all suffered, for
only those who have endured the hardest blows of fate
can overcome self and desire, to enter the way of charity

and understanding. Benassis even makes this renounce-
ment the basis of his social doctrine.

Egoism, individualism, self-interest, he declares, can
produce only social conflict. If everybody is for himself,
nobody is for the country. "Superiority is the great evil
of our age. There are more saints than there are niches
for them." Every man thinks he is better than anybody
else and more fitted to be in charge. Values have been
falsified: a small medal is good enough for a sailor who
risks his life to save a dozen others, while the highest
distinction is reserved for the politician who sells his
vote to the government. Society should rest on clear
principles and shared values, for which a man will
sacrifice his own interests. When it is based only on interests, it necessarily issues in disorder, because interests are
always in conflict, and only honour, patriotism, faith can
create unity.

It is not the passing of laws that ensures the stability of
society, but the manners and customs of its people. "A
people which has forty thousand laws has no law."
Sooner or later, to escape from this confusion, it has to
place its destiny in the hands of one man.

These long pronouncements on Balzac's social theories
are made by Benassis to an old officer of Napoleon's
whom he is taking on his rounds. This officer, devoted to
his Emperor, naturally finds them much to his liking, for
they are the sentiments of devotion which Napoleon
aroused in those who served him. This prepares the way
for *Le Napoléon du peuple* in which an old soldier speaks
of the Emperor as of a god.

Napoleon's mother had dedicated him to God, with a
vow that he would restore religion. But he had himself
almost divine power, and instances are given of his
charmed life among bullets which killed all around him,
his indifference to fatigue and lack of sleep, his immunity
to plagues that destroyed regiments. He was "the Saviour

of France." Even his journey into Egypt evokes a parallel with the Gospel story.

Finally he was betrayed like the Son of Man and martyred in St. Helena by the abominable English, for whom the officer listening to the old soldier's recital has a bitter hatred.

Yet Louis-Philippe was trying to introduce an English system of government into France. There could be no graver condemnation of him. The only kind words spoken of Louis-Philippe come from Rivet the haberdasher in *La Cousine Bette:*

> I adore Louis-Philippe. He is my god, for he is the splendid and worthy representative of the class on which he based his dynasty, and I'll never forget what he did for haberdashers by restoring the uniforms of the National Guard.

But even he complains that, after the splendour of Napoleonic reconstruction, Louis-Philippe has neglected the Louvre: because he is a man of the Centre, he wants to see the centre of Paris tidy. Just as the Empire style survived the passing of Napoleon, a nostalgia remained for a style which has something in common with Balzac's, as this too gilds and adds sphinxes to constructions that are basically classical. It was the feeling that his regime was shabby and un-French that animated resentment against Louis-Philippe, and because Napoleon was the last representative of French glory, there was a constant hankering for him which led, even before Balzac's death, to Louis Napoleon's election as President—and later to the Second Empire.

This thirst for glory, which accorded with his own thirst for fame, was strong in Balzac and in the society he describes. It explains his sometimes exaggerated efforts to inflate a scene and a language which will hardly bear the strain. Yet Napoleon himself had a practical side and could make sober judgments, a common sense which in Balzac—or at least in his writing—is even more marked. He saw, for instance, that Napoleon's laws for the division of property would result in such small farm holdings that they would eventually become unworkable. Where he was closest to Napoleon was in regarding all institutions in terms of their social value, and that is particularly notable in his attitude towards the Church.

In *Le Médecin de campagne* Benassis speaks as a doctor and a sociologist, yet all his discourses constantly refer to religion, and he is a close ally of the village priest. When stating his religious views in the Preface to *La Comédie humaine,* Balzac first names this book:

> Man is neither good nor evil, he has instincts and inclinations. Society does not corrupt him, as Rousseau claimed, but improves and completes him, but self-interest also develops his worse leanings. Christianity, and especially Catholicism, being as I have stated in *Le Médecin de campagne,* a complete system for suppressing man's corrupt inclinations, is the greatest agent of Social Order.

All this is very Napoleonic. Balzac is making a Concordat with the Church to control his characters, as Napoleon did to rule his subjects. But this reveals their views on society more than their attitude to religion. Yet even here there was a resemblance, for Napoleon's remark, "I tell you, I know men, and Jesus Christ was not a man," offers a parallel to Balzac's vision of the Church in *Jésus Christ en Flandre,* where he sees her as the inspirer of art and thought. Both regarded religion from the standpoint of their own profession—as a leader of men or as a writer of books.

Balzac looked beyond the Church as a social institution, for this was hardly more than the Marxist view of religion as a popular drug, even if he differed from this in

thinking it a far more beneficial one than any revolution.
Along with his social regard for religion went a readiness
to accept miracles and a mysticism which rushed towards
the Infinite—if this was overcharged with "sublimity," it
was held with strong conviction.

That he managed to reconcile these diverse elements
becomes less surprising when the reconciliation is again
placed in a Napoleonic context. Napoleon, as a ruler,
could come to terms with the Church without altering or
at least without disclosing his own religious feelings, but
Balzac as a writer, having accepted the Church on
grounds not very different, could no more escape her
influence on his own vision than he could extricate himself from a Goriot or a Vautrin. They are convincing
figures, but they are also images of Balzac, who could
even assert that "the smallest details of religious practice
are necessary defences against the spirit of evil," but the
feeling behind all this is as intimately his own Swedenborgian mysticism as the reality behind a Daniel d'Arthez
is Honoré de Balzac.

In the course of his life, this fusion became as complete
as it was in his work. An interesting example of this is
Une Double famille in which Granville is married to a
puritanical bigot, so austere that she preserves her scruples even against the personal judgment of the Pope.
Balzac gives a wonderful description of her bigotry, a
passage as striking in its way as the classic account of
Pons's stomach and his passionate love for stuffed carp.
He sums up the deathly effects of bigotry in a house, the
drabness of the curtains, the horror of colour, the frustration and blankness that extends even to the ornaments
and the walls, the lamentable details of the woman's
dress. Bigotry could not be more thoroughly denounced,
yet the whole point of the story is not to justify her husband's seeking happiness with another woman but to
narrate the disaster and misanthropy in which he ends

as a result of this. This was a story that Balzac worked
over more than once, and it is evident that two different
impulses were at issue. At one moment he was horrified
by "the tyranny of false religious ideas," that Jan-
senism which had also ruined the life of the country
doctor; at another he saw the tragedy of a man with a
"double family."

It is very typical of Balzac that he should so give the
two sides of the story. "*Homo Duplex*," he was fond of
quoting, as in the preface to *Les Parents pauvres*, where
he insisted that all men and all situations have two sides
to them, like a coin. But his art was precisely numis-
matic, for it showed the two sides in a single medal.
So in his eagerness to reduce everything to unity in his
work, he made sweeping gestures which certainly
brought things together, but sometimes battered or
broke them in the heap.

So in his Preface to the whole work, having cited
Le Médecin de campagne as a witness to his views on
Christianity, he adds a reference to *Louis Lambert* where
it is shown that "there has only been one religion since
the beginning of the world." The reader who turns to
the relevant passage in *Louis Lambert* finds an essay of
a page or two on comparative religion, more confident
than convincing, in which the Hindu Trimurti is identified with the Christian Trinity, and various religious
leaders are all identified in a common doctrine.

In the same Preface Balzac rebuts charges of immor-
ality, always made against original thinkers, such as
Socrates and Jesus Christ, who were killed because they
tried to reform mankind, while Luther and Calvin, who
only tried to reform religion, died in their beds. Finally,
as a proof that he was wholly opposed to materialism,
he offered the example of *Séraphita*, "this Christian
Buddha."

A Christian Buddha is again a double image, one

which well expresses the contradiction between his belief in the Christian discipline of the Church and the theosophy implicit in his mysticism. They are again joined in a letter to Madame Hanska in which he proclaims his adherence to "the mystical Church, the Church of St. John." He often refers to St. John with special respect, which indicates his reliance on a long mystical tradition derived from the early Gnostics and revived in the eighteenth century by the Illuminism of Saint-Martin to which his mother was particularly given. In fact his reading of Saint-Martin at home combined with his enthusiasm for Swedenborg at school to produce the mysticism of *Louis Lambert*. But in later life he tended to emphasize the orthodox more than the Gnostic side of this religion. The Illuminists with their belief in the "Church of St. John"—where "the beloved disciple" figures as the apostle of an inner mystery—and in the third age of the Holy Spirit spoke the language of orthodoxy, their chief objection to the Church being the hypocrisy of an establishment which was overturned by the Revolution.

In 1830, after another revolution, the Church looked different, as it appeared to Balzac when he concluded *Jésus Christ en Flandre* with the words: "I have seen the funeral of a monarchy. It is time to defend the Church."

There were other influences at work in the Church, among them the social Catholicism of Lamennais which was not without influence on Balzac, both in *Le Médecin de campagne* and *Le Curé de village*, and while Lamennais left the Church, Lacordaire, who had collaborated with him on *L'Avenir*, remained in it. So Balzac's change of outlook was accompanied by changes in the French Church—when in 1842 he began *L'Envers de l'histoire contemporaine*, the charitable works he there described were not very different from those of Ozanam. Even their mysticism is more orthodox, for it is based on *The Imitation of Jesus Christ* (though one of the best known French versions is that of Lamennais), and Balzac praises this as a book which has a message for everybody.

Finally in 1850 he and Madame Hanska confessed and received communion before their marriage in the church of St. Barbara in Berdichev. A few months later he was dying in Paris, and had a visit from Victor Hugo who recalled Balzac's pride in his house, as he said of the adjoining church, "A turn of the key and I can be at mass. I prefer that to any garden."

It is true that Talleyrand, the ex-bishop of Autun, whom Balzac met at the Duchesse de Dino's in Touraine, died in the Church, and this is no indication of a man's earlier principles, but the religious was always one side of Balzac's double nature, and if there was something in him for Flaubert, Maupassant, and even Zola, so his vision sustained another literary strain which passed through Bourget to the more fervent pages of Bernanos and Mauriac who, in an introduction to his son's book on Balzac, interprets him in his own terms. The diversity of these interpretations shows the extent of his influence, to confirm M. Marceau's remark that all French novelists are the children of *Le Père Goriot*.

La Cousine Bette

W HEN IN 1846 Balzac settled down to his last great
work, *Les Parents pauvres*, he had already arranged five years before with a group of publishers for a
complete edition of *La Comédie humaine*, to which he
had continued to add, but with many works still unwrit-
ten he was not preparing *La Cousine Bette* as his final
masterpiece. Yet in his own and the century's forties the
conditions of his life had radically altered: in 1842 he
learned of Count Hanski's death, which at last opened
the possibility of his marriage, long planned and agreed,
and as a direct result his visit to St. Petersburg in the
following year had led to arachnitis and that deterioration
in his health that finally brought death.

The causes of both these changes were more remote,
for his devotion to Madame Hanska dated from only the
third year of his success as a writer, and the ultimate
cause of his ruined health, according to his Dr. Nacquart,
was overwork and the excessive use of coffee which kept
him awake for it—habits also of long standing.

There is then a great continuity both in his life and
his work over these years, a continuity openly proclaimed
when with *Le Père Goriot* in 1835 he had envisaged his
work as a whole, and again in 1841 when he arranged its
collected edition as *La Comédie humaine*. Some novels

showed the pressing preoccupations of his daily life, but the central inspiration was so maintained and he had so devoted himself to the unity of the whole that the question of development or "late" and "early" work is rarely of interest. His real early work was that to which he refused his name.

But if the bulk of *La Comédie humaine* can be accepted as a single work, there are differences at the extremities between one of the early masterpieces and one of the last. *Le Père Goriot* showed the fullness of his powers, as *The Pickwick Papers* showed the full genius of Dickens, but *La Cousine Bette* further reveals a fullness of life. The change is certainly much less marked than the technical development which came to Dickens with *Bleak House* and *Hard Times,* but there is some similar check on exuberance and gain in construction and realism.

Whether the ultimate result is loss or gain may be similarly answered in both cases. If austere critics prefer the later work, *The Pickwick Papers* remains the most famous novel of Dickens, *Le Père Goriot* the best known of Balzac's. Yet with Balzac the difference between the early and late work is very much less, partly owing to the greater unity of his work and its embodiment in *La Comédie humaine*—a unity for which Dickens had neither aim nor ambition—but much more because the scale and scope of *La Cousine Bette* are greater than *Goriot,* and to some it may even appear as Balzac's masterpiece.

Both books too, for all their difference in plan and treatment, have very much more in common than either have with some others, for both are remarkably free from the early "sublimity" of *Séraphita* or *Le Lys dans la vallée* and from the melodrama which survived in the late *Splendeurs et misères des courtisanes.*

Yet, if only in the figure of Rastignac, *Le Père Goriot*

has an unmistakable air of youth, for it is a young man's introduction to the pleasures, deceptions, temptations, and ambitions of Paris. *La Cousine Bette* has an inevitable effect of age for the action turns less on Bette, herself no longer young, than on the ruin and dotage of Baron Hulot, who even abandons his corset and the tinting of his hair. The last words of *Goriot* are Rastignac's bold challenge to Paris, while the last words of *Bette* are a comment on Hulot's second childhood.

The difference is less between early and late work than between youth and age. *Goriot* is a young man's book, to recall Gide's dictum that Balzac should be read young. Everything is happening for the first time, with that extra sharpness of impression that belongs to fresh experience. *Bette* has the more terrible clearness of retrospect which shows the fatal consequences of wrong decisions. Yet while *Goriot* has the force of tragedy experienced in youth, *Bette,* despite all disasters in it has more lightness and that sense of inevitable comedy in human affairs that comes only with age.

Both are set in Paris, but the outlook is so different in *Bette* that it seems almost as if Paris too has grown older. The Vauquer boardinghouse of *Goriot* is certainly not gay, but the students can forget their cares at table, animated by Vautrin at his most genial. Even Josépha's or Carabine's parties in *Bette* are wearier and more sophisticated. But the real difference in the Parisian scene is more one of district, even of height, for in *Goriot* there is often a sense of exhilaration on the Montagne St. Geneviève or open air in the Luxembourg gardens, looking down on Paris as in the end Rastignac gazes down from a height on the other bank. In *Bette* there is a constant sense of cramped and central streets, such as the blind alley near the Louvre where Bette herself is disclosed— and even Crevel's luxurious little pavillion for Valérie

Marneffe is tucked away in a corner. This was the real pre-Haussman Paris, before the city of light, yet oddly the air of the still earlier *Goriot* seems fresher and more modern, simply because it is younger. In *Bette* the sense of constriction is reinforced both by the vast number of characters and by the furniture and objects of art, for Balzac had already entered on his phase of bric-à-braco-mania—ornaments and the statues produced by Wences-las Steinbock, Bette's protégé, are important and obses-sive, while his group of Samson and Delilah has more effect on the action than some minor characters.

If *Goriot* showed Balzac's entry into Paris society only a few years before he wrote it, *Bette* recorded even more immediate impressions, for it appeared under the heading of *Les Parents pauvres,* which embraced *La Cousine Bette* and *Le Cousin Pons.* That he chose just that moment to write of poor relations indicates an understanding of their feelings intensified by the scorn and hostility of Madame Hanska's relations at the prospect of his marriage into their family. The Hanskis were of sufficient importance in Russia for the Tsar's consent to be required to a mar-riage with a foreigner, while Balzac's social scale could not even rise to the "de" which he had inserted before his name, and his glory as a writer was only an obstruction, for there is a prejudice against marriage with writers or artists—a prejudice on which Valérie plays when seducing Wenceslas from his wife. News of Balzac's debts and extravagances had also reached Russia, and when he arrived there he had to endure all the ignominies of a poor relation, without the satisfaction of marriage.

It was in these circumstances that he expressed Bette's resentment at her position of inferiority, and related how she reversed that situation by reducing the Hulots to poverty and herself acquiring influence, posi-tion, and even property. If this was poetic justice, it had a parallel in real life, for the Hanskis are now best remembered because the widow of one of them married Balzac, whose fame has only increased since his death.

How much satisfaction he achieved by handling with Grandet or Gobseck the wealth that he never amassed, by defying with Vautrin the society which never admitted his rights, or by attaining with Bette the triumph that he had failed to reach, cannot of course be estimated, but as the whole force of his desire for wealth or glory was in the imagination, it is probable that his vision of their attainment was no less powerful or joyous. For there is a strange joy in *La Cousine Bette,* as every point of view is presented with such sympathy that this goes out both to those who succeed and to those who are their victims. There is never that feeling which often occurs in tragedies, that the screw has been turned a little too far, that this is too much, that this is not real life. *La Cousine Bette* is real life in that it gives the same impression of certain qualities producing certain inevitable results, and a satisfaction, even a joy, in these results. It is more exhilarating than depressing when the idyllic happiness of Wenceslas and his Hortense is destroyed, because that idyll was based on deceit and illusion. That this division has been caused by Bette, that it is her revenge, cannot spoil this sense of justice, for she has only been able to work on their weaknesses. The whole book is sustained by this accuracy and justice in the relation between human qualities and the crises that reveal them. It creates the impression that life may be cruel or tragic, but never false to its truth—which is an exact balance between character and destiny.

Not everybody would agree that life holds this truth. Some say that only art can create this sense of order and rectitude in human experience. At least Balzac here uses that art, and gives it an astonishing resemblance to life.

The conviction imposed is the more surprising because

the gaiety which refuses to desert these grim pages arises from the fact that *Bette* is really a *Conte drolatique* told in the form of a long tragedy. Two or three of the *Contes drolatiques* had a similar plot, the escapades and discomfitures of a lecherous old man. For all the action of *Bette* turns on Baron Hulot's pursuit of women, even when he is nearly seventy, and the vast sums which they succeed in squeezing out of him. But these affairs have much greater repercussions because he is director of the War ministry, his wife is devoted to him, his son is a deputy—and an austerely honest one—and his daughter is married to an artist who has aroused the desire of his own mistress.

Hulot's graft is on such a scale that it nearly leads to a government crisis. At least it causes the death of his brother and his uncle, and nearly kills his wife. This may not appear the stuff of a *Conte drolatique,* but violence and tragedy also intervene in these stories, not only in *La Connétable* and *Le Succube,* and *Bette* remains true to them in its rapid transitions from gaiety to disaster. Nothing could be more burlesque than the scene in which Hulot and Valérie are discovered in bed by her husband and the police, yet it is precisely this comedy which sets off the crises and the deaths in Hulot's family.

Any comedy in *Goriot* is subordinate to the central theme, but the whole action of *Bette* turns on the comedy of an old man's lust which happens to have tragic consequences. Yet it remains a comedy in the sense that all tricks are in the end exposed, Crevel and Valérie and Bette all die disappointed of their hopes for the final ruin of the Hulots, who are restored to their possessions and even to happiness, their characters strengthened—with one exception. This exception, Baron Hulot himself, underlines the comedy, for he is the incorrigible pantaloon who even in his dotage returns to his old tricks.

The construction has all the intricacy necessary to a long sustained comedy. *Bette* is the longest of Balzac's novels, for *Illusions perdues* and *Splendeurs et misères des courtisanes* are both divided into parts more or less complete in themselves, but *Bette* maintains a central theme for over five hundred pages without chapters, without even a break, though it covers a period of over six years—and the transitions of time hardly interrupt the flow of the narrative. The contrast here with the shorter *Goriot*, whose action only begins after fifty pages of description, is very marked, for *Bette*'s begins on the first page.

Constantly, but especially after the marriage of Wenceslas and Hortense, incident, action, movement are accelerated, as Hulot turns to more desperate expedients for money, and Valérie Marneffe convinces four men that they are the father of the child she bears, delights them—and gives great satisfaction to her husband who, being employed at Hulot's War ministry, sees in this a prospect of further promotion.

This is, of course, an essentially comic, almost theatrical situation, with fathers, lovers, and husband entering and disappearing through doors on opposite sides of the stage (and in fact the Brazilian Baron Montès de Montejanos is at one moment concealed in a closet). But the trick is managed with extraordinary art, as the transitions are effected by Valérie with immense skill. It is amusing, but it is not farcical, for even while making Valérie witty, attractive, and intelligent, Balzac never conceals her essential depravity. Only a supreme comic gift, on the scale of a Molière who could similarly balance contrasts with a double sympathy—as with Alceste and Célimène—is able to handle such a situation.

What is most striking is how much Balzac can afford to do with his characters, he who in earlier days was constantly on the edge of the sublime and the ridiculous.

Here, as if to show with a flourish that he had solved that particular problem, he deliberately puts one of his most "sublime" characters in the most ridiculous light—and she emerges without the loss of a feather from her "angelic" wings. Adeline is the noblest and most devoted of wives and mothers, yet she is shown as attractive from the first pages when Crevel tries to seduce her, and she is so uncomplaining that one can share the surprise of Hulot's brother that he should prefer any woman to her. One can even understand the momentary impulse of generosity in the pompous and selfish Crevel when he later promises to find the large sum she requires for Hulot's debts and to demand nothing in return.

But on his way to raise this money, Crevel visits his Valérie, who is naturally affronted to find him deeply moved by the appeal of another woman. So she reveals her own religious feelings, herself becomes "sublime," and reduces him to tears—whereupon she bursts out laughing and tells him how easy it is. If he is so anxious to part with his money, she can make appeals even more sublime than those of Adeline—and she is also younger and more skilled in the art of pleasing. Crevel capitulates at once, and saves his capital. Adeline's appeal is forgotten.

The art of this is that while Crevel is convinced, the reader is not. Balzac makes him aware that Adeline is right and Valérie wrong. Here at last the sublime can suffer the worst ridicule, that of caricature, and remain sublime. Balzac had immense confidence to dare such a scene, and it is this mastery which is evident throughout the book.

The chief differences in technique, as compared with earlier work, are the swifter entry into action from the first page, more unity of action and plot, increased use of dialogue. All these are points essential to a piece on the stage, and it is likely that Balzac's experiments in the theatre had contributed to this development. In 1840 his *Vautrin* had been played at the Porte Saint-Martin, but had been suppressed by the government chiefly because the famous Lemaître had given an impression of Louis-Philippe in his part. Neither *Pamela Giraud* nor *Les Ressources de Quinola* won success, which came only with *La Marâtre* in 1848, two years after *Bette,* but was again impeded by Louis-Philippe, this time by the revolution against him. The greatest success, *Mercadet,* was posthumous: this was a comedy of debt, in which Mercadet puts off creditors by insisting on waiting for Godeau, a partner from whom he really expects nothing. But in the end the almost mythical Godeau returns— with all the wealth required.

La Cousine Bette already contains this promise of ultimate success in the theatre, and it too is a comedy of debt finally redeemed. For Victorin Hulot, the old man's son, eventually has recourse to the police—he even has a brief glimpse of Vautrin as chief of police—but it is Vautrin's aunt, Madame Nourrison, a private operator, who restores the Hulots' fortunes by killing off Crevel and Valérie shortly after their marriage. This too is a theatrical stroke, and even Valérie's death has a comic element as she tries to seduce Heaven with the arts which have served her so well on earth: *il faut que je fasse le bon Dieu.* So the dying Crevel remains pompous and comic:

> Death will think twice before tackling a mayor of Paris
> . . . and if my ward is unfortunate enough to lose the man
> it has twice honoured with its suffrages—ah, note the
> facility with which I frame my sentences—well, I shall
> know how to pack up. I've been a commercial traveller,
> I know when to move on.

Even more comic are the doctors in conference over the tropical disease which has struck both Crevel and his wife. Bianchon, greatest of doctors, preserves his dignity and his sympathy, but one of his colleagues cannot help drawing attention to their good fortune:

> It will be a magnificent autopsy, for we'll have the two of them and we'll be able to compare the cases in detail.

Few writers dare to make these brusque transitions between the comic and the tragic, which occur so naturally in real life, where the stomach or the bladder show a strange indifference to style by intervening in the solemnities of love or death. Balzac himself had not often made them with such complete ease and mastery. Here he passes lightly enough from the Church, "animated by the spirit of sacrifice in everything" offering to the heap of decaying flesh on the bed "her infinite care and her inexhaustible treasures of mercy"—to the prospect of the "splendid autopsy."

Many of the most powerful effects in his work are obtained by contrast, for his greatest felicities are always in the double face of the coin—his *Homo Duplex*—and he is least successful when he keeps too continuously to one level, especially the "sublime" as in *Séraphita*. He is most successful when he uses his double vision, which could see the tragedy in the lightest love and the comedy in the tragic moment, even in death. If on his own deathbed he called for Bianchon, who had been unable to save Crevel and Valérie, that was not only because he was entering the world of his own vision, but because that vision had irony in its roots.

This irony is present throughout *La Cousine Bette,* where it serves to control the exuberance to which his characters were always liable, owing to their heritage of his own rich blood. When Hortense, betrayed by Wenceslas, declares that she is unable to copy the wonderful example of her mother's submission to an erring husband, and says that she is more a Hulot than a Fischer, she

reveals even more that she is a Balzac. Yet even she,
and even her "sublime" mother are here well under the
control of Balzac's irony, for he admits the limitations
of this noblest of women, to whom Josépha says that if
she had a little of their *chic*, she would have kept her
husband at home, "for you would have been what we
have to be, *all women* for one man."

Balzac controls the exuberance of his characters, and
even limits the exuberance of his comment, but this
question of comment has to be seen against the whole
background of his work, which is rarely quite free from
it. That his comments are excessive, that they disrupt
the realism of his work, are the two criticisms most
commonly urged against Balzac. His intrusive personality, his lack of discretion, show most clearly in these
comments.

The justice in this criticism may obscure three different points. First, he is sometimes even more present in
the centre of action, in a Goriot or even, as Henry
James noted, in a Renée or her child. Second, in writing
a history of manners, a social study, it was often necessary for him to comment. Third, these comments are intelligent, acute, exactly adapted to their subject, of
which they are not only an integral part, but on occasion
the most interesting part.

After Balzac, the influence of Flaubert, strong on
Henry James and on Conrad, eliminated comment from
the novel, which was held to be an exact transcription of
life, an illusion only impeded by the intruding of an
author's personality or opinions. Yet there is a more
important illusion than this, that precisely of being in
touch with the personality of an author dead or distant.
The voice of Henry James, however discreet, remains
unmistakable, even because it is so discreet. So Balzac's
comments are no more and no less himself than his

presence in a Félix de Vandenesse or a Louise de Macumer. The ultimate question is always whether the author is acceptable in himself, for he is present in his technique as in his style.

It remains true that Balzac also tended to eliminate comment in his later work, but in *La Cousine Bette,* which was nearly his last, there remain between half a dozen and a dozen passages, mostly only a paragraph, but one of two pages, that may be taken as comments undemanded by the action, though some are required to elucidate a character. It is also true that among them are some of the best passages in the book, and the longest is essential to an understanding not only of Wenceslas but of Balzac himself.

This is the great passage in which he declares that intellectual work is one of the greatest efforts possible to mankind, demanding courage above all other qualities, for without that there is no passing from vision to creation:

> To think, dream, conceive great works is a fine occupation. It is like smoking enchanted cigars, or surrendering like a woman to her lover. . . . The man who can put his plan into words already has some reputation. Yet all artists and writers have this gift. But give birth to the child, put it to bed each night satisfied, embrace it every morning with tenderness, caress it when it's filthy, find it new clothes which it is always tearing to pieces . . . that's the real task. The hand has to be ready at every moment to obey the head. But the head can no more command its creative powers than love can survive without rest.

The bitterness of experience is confirmed by another phrase: work is begun in despair and abandoned in grief. Doubtless this is Balzac's experience, but it is here applied very aptly to the Polish sculptor Wenceslas, who, spoiled by the fondness of his wife, falls back on "the enchanted cigars": "Instead of a statue, a charming little Wenceslas was brought into the world."

Another passage, earlier in the book, observes that the vicious often have more charm than the virtuous, because they put themselves out to please more, to cover up their faults. Though this is offered as a general comment, it explains how Hulot is loved despite his vices, and it is justified by his wife's offer of her diamonds to pay the expense of his mistress: his reply that the diamonds are to be kept for their daughter Hortense at once strikes his wife as noble and self-sacrificing.

So another comment on the grandeur of virginity explains the extraordinary force of character in Bette herself. Virgin natures economize their vital powers which enable them in a crisis to surmount difficulties with a greater strength. Virginity is "a grandiose and terrible exception," deserving all the honours of religion. It is typical of Balzac that this rhapsody on virginity should be provoked by Bette exactly at the moment when she plans the ruin of the Hulots. He has the same justice to her as towards Hulot, not extenuating their faults but even less concealing their virtues, for his vision is their own, and few are quite blind to their own virtues. Certainly his mercy is on all his works.

A comment aroused by Valérie Marneffe is more social in scope—he is here "the secretary of French society"—for he observes that married women who take lovers, usually with the connivance of their husbands, are more dangerous in their hypocrisy than any courtesan such as Josépha or Carabine, who treat men honestly in their trade. Valérie pretends to be "a poor weak woman," a martyr to passion, an ideal love. This new romantic love, says Balzac, offers the whole Gospel to the service of the Devil.

Two other comments return to one of the main themes in *La Cousine Bette,* the difficulty of finding a mistress and a wife in the same woman. That the answer in the two cases is different shows how closely these comments are incorporated in the narrative, for in one case the man's failure is considered as the cause, in the second the woman's. The first context is a woman's reflection, the second a man's. Here again is the double vision:

> Many men want two editions of the same work, though it is an immense sign of a man's inferiority if he is unable to make a mistress of his wife. Variety is a mark of impotence. Constancy is always the genius of love, revealing the true power of a poet.

The second:

> Love, which is both a great folly and the austere joy of great souls, and pleasure, which is sold in the market-place, are two different aspects of the same fact. The woman able to satisfy these two contrasted demands is as rare as a great general, writer, artist, or inventor.

Balzac adds, recognising a contrast in such comments, that there is more than one sort of morality in his work—and this is surely the reason why his comments are not more resented, for they are not a set of prejudices or principles imposed on life without reference to particular cases: they arise from those cases, and came from the same inspiration in his own mind. They are in fact an integral part of his vision.

La Cousine Bette is an outstanding example of that vision's unity, of the unity in his whole work. Other characters of *La Comédie humaine* appear in it, some only mentioned by name, but all help to create a special atmosphere—Rastignac, Nucingen, Bixiou, the Duc d'Hérouville, Madame de la Chanterie, Jenny Cadine—even the great Vautrin, though his name is hardly more than whispered. Others play more important, though still minor roles, among them Bianchon who, called in for Adeline, reveals that he is also attending Valérie, her husband's former mistress—and Valérie herself is the natural daughter of Montcornet, who occurs in five other novels. So all the references cross, to form a unity not only in *La Cousine Bette*, but in *La Comédie humaine* itself.

La Comédie humaine

W HEN BALZAC wanted an image for *La Comédie hu-maine*, he chose Bourges cathedral—it would, he told Madame Hanska, bulk as large in literature as Bourges in architecture. Marcel Bouteron, the dean of Balzac studies, developed this image to show how different features, a flying buttress or a chapel, could yet form part of an artistic unity, though built in different centuries, even in different styles.

Some such image may be required to illustrate how ninety different pieces, some of them long novels, and over two thousand characters, can compose an artistic whole. Balzac in his resolve to create a history of manners emphasized his system, but the unity of *La Comédie humaine* is hardly that of a system. Its strength is precisely that of a natural growth, and in fact it grew naturally, for it was not until 1835, the year of *Goriot*, when Balzac had already been writing for five years works which were to form part of it, that he had a vision of the integration of characters in the whole, though according to his sister he had conceived the plan in the previous year.

After that, testimonies multiply, from Henry Reeve, an Englishman who declared that Balzac expounded the plan to him in 1835, Reeve himself remarking that a Diobolic Comedy would be the proper name for the whole work, to that of Félix Davin, who in the same year wrote of "this great history of man and Society which M. de Balzac is preparing for us."

From the beginning Balzac had held to the philosophical value of his work, and in fact the *Études philosophiques* were some of the earliest, while both *La Peau de chagrin* and *Le Médecin de campagne* with all its social doctrine were early works, and still earlier was an *Étude analytique, Physiologie du mariage.* Then his short stories in 1830 had been published as *Scènes de la vie privée.* All in fact lay ready to his hand when he made the great discovery that he was writing not pieces but a masterpiece.

In 1841 his publishers declared:

> Intelligent readers will not have waited until today to realise that M. de Balzac had conceived, from the beginning of his career as a writer, a vast plan in which each of his novels was to be, in a sense, no more than a detached scene.

This says too much, for only *Scènes de la vie privée* indicated that, and to emphasize the early origin of the plan is to obscure its natural growth. *La Comédie humaine* has the unity of a forest which was not planted, but grew as Balzac's genius expanded. One or two discrepancies exist to confirm this. In the final arrangement it is not easy to follow the distinction between *Scènes de la vie privée* and *Scènes de la vie parisienne,* for *Le Père Goriot* and other shorter pieces, such as *Madame Firmiani,* which appear in the first are even more Parisian than some such as *La Duchesse de Langeais* or *Facino Cane* which appear in the second. Again not all the *Études philosophiques* are more philosophical than stories which appear elsewhere—they have to appear there because they belong nowhere else, being set in other centuries and even in other countries.

The reason for both these discrepancies surely lies in the fact that both the *Scènes de la vie privée* and some of the *Études philosophiques* had been written before it occurred to Balzac that he was really writing *La Comédie humaine*. These are exactly the discrepancies, similar to knots in timber or curves in a river, which occur in natural growths, but not in works ordered on a set intellectual plan. Balzac certainly conceived a plan, but it is less certain that he worked according to plan, for he made room without difficulty for works conceived later. This again was natural enough, for plan and works both emerged from the same head.

There are more discrepancies even in the Catalogue adopted in 1845 for a complete edition in twenty-six volumes. This, for instance, contains eight titles in the *Scènes de la vie politique,* only half of which were ever written, while the *Scènes de la vie militaire* contain no less than twenty-three items, only two of which were written (Balzac wrote to Stendhal that he had been discouraged here by the magnificent description of the Battle of Waterloo in *La Chartreuse de Parme*). More surprising still, even at that late date, when his health was already failing, he found time to write six works not included in the Catalogue, among them one of his greatest, *La Cousine Bette*. This shows clearly enough that he never allowed the splendour of the plan to cramp his style, nor to smother inspirations not directly demanded by the system. This again confirms the natural growth of the whole.

If he had written the same number of novels and stories in which characters reappeared, his work would have been much the same and as much a unity without the title of *La Comédie humaine,* which is simply his collected works, exclusive of the *Contes drolatiques*, described as an "arabesque" decoration around the main work, appropriate to what he had called the Arabian Nights of the West. The fantasy is more striking than the system.

The reason why a single title was necessary to the whole was in his own character. He was claiming a higher status for the novel than it had yet attained, and he was naturally irritated when a work as serious as *La Peau de chagrin* was dismissed as an entertainment. He was also more philosophical in his early work—*Séraphita*, *Le Médecin de campagne*, *Louis Lambert* were all written before the main plan had been decided—and he rightly felt that they were worth more serious consideration than was usually given to novels then. But he remained a novelist, and in fact his later development led him away from this philosophical trend to the pure novel, culminating in *La Cousine Bette*.

So, while still in the philosophical phase, yet with the murmur of future novels already in his head, he chose the title of *Études sociales* for the work planned, to combine the two impulses, and also no doubt to impress the publishers and the public. In this there was more of his exuberance, his dandyism, his fantasy than respect for system. What really impressed the public was *Le Père Goriot*, not the heading under which it appeared.

The actual title of *La Comédie humaine* came later. Its appearance in print was in 1841, but it is possible that Balzac, who often had Dante in mind (*Les Proscrits*, in which Dante figures, is one of his earliest stories), thought of it long before, and he had travelled in Italy for the Viscontis. One of his dedications is to a Cajetani prince who is praised for his Dante scholarship. It is even possible that Reeve's comment of a Diabolic Comedy, back in 1835, aroused some meditation, and "Diabolic" was rejected as an English puritan gloss.

What is more interesting in Reeve's account is that the three divisions which he says Balzac mentioned to him were those retained in the final arrangement, *Études de mœurs, Études philosophiques, Études analytiques.* Yet they remain more a fine prospectus than a helpful guide to the work. This becomes clear when it is seen that the *Études de mœurs* occupy four-fifths of the whole work. They are themselves divided into *Scènes*—the word which has belonged to the first collection of stories to bring him fame—under six heads: private life, Parisian, provincial, political, military, and country life.

Of these the scenes of private and Parisian life occupy between them nearly half of the total work. The disproportion again shows how little he allowed an artificial plan to check the natural bent of his mind. Living in Paris, which was then not only a centre of Europe but of the world, it was natural that he should write chiefly of Paris, and most of the scenes of private life either happened there or refer to it. So nearly half of *La Comédie humaine* is Parisian in inspiration.

That Paris inspired so much justifies the great rhapsody at the beginning of *Ferragus* over "the very complete monster":

> He who has never admired your dark landscapes, your flashes of light, your long and silent blind alleys, nor heard the things you whisper between midnight and two in the morning, knows nothing of your real poetry, your strange and striking contrasts. There is a select body of admirers who always have their wits about them and who savour their Paris . . . Paris is a real person, as every man, every corner of a house, is a living tissue of this great courtesan whose head, heart, and fantastic behaviour are perfectly familiar to them. They are the true lovers of Paris. . . .

That is in every sense the capital point of *La Comédie humaine,* but Balzac was far from uncritical in his appreciation of Paris, and this passage from *Ferragus* needs to be balanced by one which introduces *La Fille aux yeux d'or*:

> One of the most terrible sights there is to see is the appearance of people in Paris, the horror of their gaunt, pale, sallow faces . . . less faces than masks, masks of weakness or strength, masks of misery or joy, masks of hypocrisy . . . almost infernal in hue, for it is not lightly that Paris has been called a hell. . . .
>
> In Paris no feeling can resist the course of events which sweeps all into a conflict of passions. Love there is no more than desire, hatred a whim, the only reliable relation is a thousand franc note, the only friend a pawnbroker. The general current has its effects on all, for indoors as in the street nobody is quite out of place, nobody wholly useful nor wholly harmful—fools and idlers, the intelligent and the honest. Everything is tolerated there, the government and the guillotine, religion and cholera.

This contrast may seem one more example of the double face that Balzac found in things, but in fact the two passages treat not quite the same subject, for the first relates to Paris, the second to the people of Paris, and as is usual with Balzac, the place is described with exuberance, the people with irony, even with bitterness.

It is true that romantic poets from Wordsworth to Keats or Lamartine to Vigny find more to raise their spirits in the beauty of nature and more to depress them in mankind or the dilemmas of human destiny. Prospects pleased them, but men were vile. Yet this was not the division between places and people in Balzac. It was not nature, but towns, the creation of men and women, which inspired him, and because he lived inside the people of his world, he had what was almost self-indulgence for them—so much that he was often accused of encouraging vice. He was less struck by the vileness of men than fascinated by the obstinacy of their desires and ambitions.

His vision of people was not a contrast to his vision of places but an extension of it, for as he noted the effect of Paris on faces in the street, so in all his work he looked for the effect of place and the callings peculiar to it on character. If half the *Études de mœurs*, which were the bulk of his work, were mostly inspired by Paris, whether under the heading of Parisian or of private life, the remaining four heads—provincial, political, military, and country life—were hardly less inspired by the spirit of place.

This is obvious enough in the scenes of provincial life, where the Nemours of *Ursule Mirouet*, the Alençon of *Une Vieille fille*, the Angoulême of *Illusions perdues* are so lovingly described. But it is hardly less true of the scenes of country life, the Limousin of *Le Curé de village*, the Burgundy of *Les Paysans*, or the Dauphiné of *Le Médecin de campagne*. One of the reasons why the other two sections, the scenes of political and of military life, remained the most incomplete was that, for all his efforts, Balzac had never entered political life—two years before his death he failed to enter the Assembly, and as he had not been there to see, his vision lacked a stimulus—while for the scenes of military life he had projected a tour of the Napoleonic battlefields which he was unable to undertake.

Even in the *Études philosophiques*, locality was no less important: the wonderful description of Flanders at the beginning of *Le Recherche de l'absolu*, of Venice in *Massimilla Doni*, Le Croisic in *Un Drame au bord de la mer*—and strangest of all, as he had never been there, the Norway of *Séraphita*. This shows that although place was most often the element that stimulated his vision, it was the vision itself, not direct observation, that lay at the basis of his work.

If then the imposing headings of *La Comédie humaine*, designed to give the impression of a philosophical work or a social treatise, resolve themselves largely into a list of places and provinces, and mostly ones that he had visited, they had some other value for Balzac. The philosophical and social values were real, but the headings were chiefly to assert this point in face of a public not yet prepared to treat the novel with the seriousness it has since attained. For himself the value of a framework was that, though he broke out of it often enough as the discrepancies noted above make clear, it served to limit his vision, to check the exuberance of his powers.

What is most daunting to a young man once conscious of his powers is the immense scope offered by the spectacle of the world. He is oppressed by the terrible burden of his freedom. He may decide, like Balzac, that he is going to be a great man, even that he is going to be a great writer, yet still be overwhelmed by the vast choice not only of material but of style and form. A first attempt is often at poetry, regarded as the quintessence of literature, and Balzac began with a drama in verse, *Cromwell.* Its failure stopped that outlet. So in his early unsigned work he gradually eliminated more possibilties until he found his true form, not perhaps in *Les Chouans,* though he signed it, but in *La Peau de chagrin* and the *Scènes de la vie privée.* Yet even *La Peau de chagrin* was a tempting line of fantasy which had to be controlled, and it was only with *Goriot* that he set the limits which he needed in the discovery that his books were all to be about the same people who would recur throughout them—over two thousand, but all related in their common relationship to himself.

The limits were so successful that to some critics, such as Professor Lukács, Balzac and Tolstoy are the only true classical realists in the history of the novel. That is one point from which to view Balzac, but even in the years immediately before and after *Goriot* he was also writing the *Contes drolatiques,* as if feeling the need to expand an exuberance to which he had already set limits—though in fact his comic genius also animated *La Comédie humaine*.

Once the limits are acknowledged, those of his own world with Paris as its centre, its provinces as securely based on existing towns, it is astonishing how many characters and types he managed to crowd into it. It is not only that many French provinces are represented with their inhabitants—Touraine and Normandy are each the background of seven stories, Brittany of three—but foreigners also enter, drawn as ever to Paris: the Brazilian Montès de Montejanos, the Portuguese Ajuda-Pinto, the lover of Madame de Beauséant, the Spanish Baron de Macumer and the terrible Spaniards of *El Verdugo*, Schmucke, the German musician of *Le Cousin Pons*, Facino Cane and the Italians of *Sarrasine* and *Gambara*, the English Lady Dudley or Arthur Grenville in *Le Femme de trente ans*, the Pole Wenceslas Steinbock and the more heroic Pole of *La Fausse maîtresse*, Corsicans such as those of *La Vendetta*—and Napoleon, one of the few historical characters that Balzac retained, for most he eliminated, finding that his own had stronger claims to represent his world.

Yet it is not these foreigners, though they show the range of his mind, who are the true natives of Balzac's world, nor the other great exceptions, a Goriot and a Claes whose passions are so absolute that these destroy them in the scenes where they first appear. Those who form the unity of *La Comédie humaine* are minor characters in the novels, but by the frequency of their reappearance major characters in the work as a whole—Bianchon, Nucingen, Bridau, Lousteau, Maxime de Trailles, de Marsay, Diane de Maufrigneuse, Madame d'Espard, Jenny Cadine, and many others. Rastignac and Félix de Vandenesse might head the list, but they are the only two recurring characters who are also central figures in major works, though others have shorter stories which they dominate, Diane in *Les Secrets de la Princesse de Cadignan*, de Marsay in *La Fille aux yeux d'or*, while Bridau has a greater role in *La Rabouilleuse*, but Rastignac is a case apart, for with fifteen appearances he is not only with de Marsay one of the most recurring figures but also, as the central character of *Goriot*, one with a biography of his own.

Yet Bianchon, with twenty-three appearances, surpasses even Rastignac. These two, the students in *Goriot*, in which Balzac first adopted the device of recurring characters, best illustrate the part played by this in the whole work. Such characters serve both as points of reference and as points of interest, for they are both useful, almost conventional abbreviations, as the reader at once knows what sort of a person is one who has Rastignac for a friend, and stimulants, for there is a desire to know what has since happened to Rastignac himself. The device reinforces the illusion of real life, as in the recognition of a familiar face, and arouses curiosity, as in the desire for the latest news.

Dr. Hunt, in a witty comment on Balzac's courtesans, recalls William of Ockham's principle that entities should not be multiplied beyond reason. If Balzac had to multiply courtesans, so swiftly supplanted, ravaged, or even respectably retired in Paris that their lives there were too brief for the time sequence of *La Comédie humaine*, he was able to use more restraint over other characters, such as a Bianchon whose medical career could usefully extend over a whole generation. Yet his reputation was soon too great for trivial cases: "It's a case for Bianchon" at once conveys the gravity of a condition. The personal touch carries much more conviction than any account of symptoms. So when Lucien makes the acquaintance of Rastignac, it is at once more evident that he is winning a name for himself in Paris than any details of his earnings or his clothes could establish. By the date of *Illusions perdues* a man had to be somebody to know Rastignac.

These recurring characters briefly indicate a social milieu, cutting short details of houses and furniture, for it is sufficient to note that a woman is accepted by Madame d'Espard or Madame de Sérizy to know what her own salon will be like.

They also carry financial implications: the names of Nucingen and du Tillet introduce a mileau of high finance without scruple but inside the law, while a Claparon is charged with their shadier transactions. So a Popinot stands for commercial honesty, a Granville for justice. When the unfortunate Colonel Chabert, long missing and believed dead on the battlefield of Eylau—his wife has even remarried—tries to establish his identity, it is a capital point in his story that he goes to Derville, one of the few honest lawyers in Paris. That even Derville cannot save him points the tragedy of his fate—if he had applied to the Fraisier who so swindled Pons it would have been no more than bad luck. So there is hope for Birotteau once the illustrious Gaudissart is in charge of the publicity for his hair tonic, so there is hope for Lucien when he accepts advice from d'Arthez, fear when he listens to Lousteau.

For Balzac, in the extravagance of his invention, these recurring characters were a great economy. They set limits to his vision, which had quite enough characters in view. It was both useless and inartistic for him to create more lawyers or journalists, when he already had these to hand. As he entered ever more intensely into his world, he could no more think of using others than a man in a crisis will be content with any but his own doctor, his own lawyer. He too was living in a world of his own where both loyalty and common sense demanded that he should appeal only to his trusted advisers.

It is this which best justifies the claim of *La Comédie humaine* to be a single work, not simply a collection of books—they are "books" only in the sense of the old epics, all parts of one great chant. For characters recur as in legends, the paladins of Charlemagne in Ariosto or the knights of Arthur in Malory.

Because it had this quality of a legend, *La Comédie humaine* won popularity, and Balzac, despite all the importance he attached to the philosophical and social value of his work, was always hoping to rival the sales of Dumas. This too was why the Napoleonic legend was so firmly embedded in his work. The old soldier who tells the story of *Le Napoléon du peuple* even insists that the Emperor is not dead . . . like Arthur, like Barbarossa.

Political scientists may judge Napoleon differently, sociologists give a different interpretation to Balzac, but one of the strengths of *La Comédie humaine* is that it has lifted this legend from the deceptions of history into the truth of art. M. Claude Mauriac has said that he began to think more favourably of the statesman Thiers when he heard that Rastignac might owe something to him. So a prejudice against Napoleon might be revised by *La Comédie humaine,* because he behaves so indulgently to Laurence de Cinq-Cygne when she appeals to him on the eve of Jena in *Une Ténébreuse affaire.* This is the victory of art, that historical figures may owe more to it than to their own achievements. The myth is stronger than the fact.

Marcel Bouteron puts this well when he says:

> We have known men of ambition, brutes, and rakes, but their reality pales before that of Rastignac, Philippe Bridau, old Hulot. By making such types as these constantly recur through all the variety of action in *La Comédie humaine,* Balzac obsesses us with their figures. . . .

Because Balzac's recurring characters have this obsessive quality, his readers become more addicts than admirers, and *La Comédie humaine* more a club than a piece of literature. With even more fervour than those who debate the private life of Sherlock Holmes, followers of Balzac discuss the affairs of Diane de Maufrigneuse, the career of Rastignac, the interventions of Lady Dudley, or the last incarnation of Vautrin. Scholars have compiled admirable inventories of these characters from the Cerfberr and Christophe repertory of *La Comédie humaine* in 1887 to M. Fernand Lotte's more recent biographical dictionary of persons in it. All are accounted for, from the most recurring to those who put in the briefest appearance, to form an encyclopaedia, as Bouteron has called *La Comédie humaine*.

This encyclopaedia remains fantastic and human, as it endears characters by their sudden reappearance. Even so slight an anecdote as *Étude de femme* becomes important simply because M. de Listomère glances up from his paper to say: "I see that Madame de Mortsauf is dead." With a shock one is taken back to the ending of *Le Lys dans la vallée* . . . as again in *Une Fille d'Ève* when one meets the Félix of that novel married . . . and then his brother appears in *La Femme de trente ans.* So the whole world assumes the ease and casualness of a conversation with its startled comments: "I had no idea that you knew her . . . what is she doing now?"

These characters have a greater interest than acquaintances because more is known about the intimate crises of their lives. It is precisely Balzac's realism that makes his world fantastic. In real life a man's trade, his heart, his income, his religion, his mind are known in different circles, and it is rarely that any one person stands at the centre of all these circles. By revealing interrelationships in a whole society, Balzac disclosed a new vision of life,

one attempted by no other novelist with so large a focus.
Yet his remains a fantastic world just because it is so complete. More novels are written from a single point of
view, either that of the novelist, or of the character in
whom he has placed himself. Balzac's point of view has
four thousand eyes. It is this which makes *La Comédie
humaine* appear monstrous or prodigious.

The novelist has freedom to extend his sympathy towards all who are in reach of his understanding. Nobody
has used that freedom of sympathy with more audacity
than Balzac. More recent writers have engaged sympathy
for sexual or criminal eccentrics, but usually without
attempting at the same time to arouse sympathy for more
central characters. Vautrin was both a criminal and a
sexual eccentric, but he was only one of an immense
range of characters for whom Balzac succeeds in arous-
ing sympathy.

Size and range are not greatness, but when a writer
rises above a certain level, the breadth of his view is
some witness to the power of his vision. Men of small
output, however exquisite, are rarely accepted as masters,
if only because they have not left posterity enough to
learn from them. The bulk of *La Comédie humaine* is not
its first claim to greatness, but it contains enough great
work between *Le Père Goriot* and *La Cousine Bette* to
stimulate and sustain interest in the rest of the family.

Lord R'hoone

BALZAC'S GREATNESS is widely acknowledged, yet there is more disagreement about its quality. He remains as awkward a figure as when he first achieved fame in Paris—and as open to caricature and misrepresentation. He is an embarrassment even to encyclopaedias and histories of literature which require a brief and accepted formula such as has not yet been found for him . . . "powerful . . . genius . . . complete picture of French society . . . observation . . . imagination. . . ." That is hardly enough, the difficulty being that few care to place him in relation to other novelists. Lesser writers may be granted some well-judged comparison, but not Balzac.

Yet M. André Maurois and Mr. Somerset Maugham, orthodox spokesmen of French and English writing, are content simply to call him the greatest of novelists. In face of this, it is necessary to enquire why such a claim is not universally accepted.

It is not enough to repeat Lamartine's remark that he was a great man to whom the fates were mean, for they remain mean over a century after his death, and persistent ill luck is often related to a man's character. A writer's chances in the halls of fame often depend on a constant appeal to an enduring principle which he exemplifies for posterity. Here is the difficulty, that posterity has not yet decided just where Balzac stands.

What used to be a political and religious difficulty has become one of criticism and psychology. In the past, even the fervour of some supporters has often discouraged others, for conservatives and Marxists, Catholics and theosophists, nationalists and cosmopolitans have been disconcerted by their opponents. Similar controversies over Shakespeare are dismissed to the prejudice of the opinionated, but those over Balzac appear more often to discredit him, because he has neither the status nor the aloofness of a Shakespeare.

A great man, if he is not to represent a principle, is often held to stand for his country or his age. Here again Balzac has been unfortunate, for he was not only refused a place in the French Academy, but has never quite achieved that undisputed glory in France which belongs of right to a Rabelais, a Molière, or a Racine. Since the Revolution, France has been so passionately divided between its supporters and opponents, or anticlericals and clericals, that each side has been at one time or another exasperated by Balzac, whose Bonapartism (though it has something in common with De Gaulle's France) was discredited by the collapse of the Second Empire. But there is a more important element in Balzac's own character, his simple exuberance and the child in him, which arouses more mockery in Paris than elsewhere. His contemporaries found it hard to take him seriously, and many of their descendants remain in the same difficulty. A great Frenchman has above all to be *digne*—and Balzac endured many indignities.

If he is not wholly acceptable to his country, still less can he be held to represent his age, when it was that of Louis-Philippe which he so cordially detested.

Yet today the worst controversy is in literary criticism, over his place in the history of the novel and over his

style. Here again he is often more appreciated abroad
than in France, where literary vendettas can be Corsican
in their intensity. The same sobriety which demanded a
respect for the unities in the drama has imposed a similar
restraint on the novel, to form a tradition of which the
most accepted exponents are Choderlos de Laclos,
Stendhal, Flaubert, Proust, and even Colette. Balzac
might have found a place in that tradition if he had
written only *Le Curé de Tours* and *Eugénie Grandet,* but
the rest of his work proved how little he really belonged
to it.

This tradition insists most on a certain sobriety of
style, and it is for his faults of style than Balzac has most
often been condemned. Certainly his language was sometimes inflated, but that could be a fault in Shakespeare,
to whom all the romantic school looked for inspiration.
Nor is it just to set Stendhal against Balzac, who almost
alone saluted his *Chartreuse de Parme* as a masterpiece.
Stendhal, neglected in his day, was astonished by the
praise which, he said, he had not expected for another
century when people would still be reading *Le Père
Goriot.* It is true that Stendhal also maintained that
Balzac's style could be pruned with advantage, and even
suspected that he added romantic flourishes to it. Yet,
as Professor Lukács points out, it is only Balzac's style
which has romantic lapses, and Stendhal's heroes are
much more romantic than his. It is even the romanticism
of a Julien Sorel and a Fabrice del Dongo, their lonely
defiance of the world, which has so endeared Stendhal to
modern taste, as it was only his style which prevented his
recognition in his own day. That Balzac himself admired
it showed that his own view was more comprehensive.

Even in France, it is no longer generally maintained
that Balzac wrote badly. In asserting this, M. Philippe
Bertault quotes as the wisest estimate of his style the
remark of Taine, that Balzac understood the spirit of

the language, understood it better than anybody, but simply used it in his own manner. That this manner was not always acceptable to a particular French tradition may no more affect his position in world literature than it is necessary to be a Norwegian to appreciate Ibsen. Many of the criticisms directed against Balzac were made against Dickens in England, even when his fame was secure in the outside world.

Stefan Zweig, in comparing Balzac and Dickens, was struck by a similarity in the publics to which they appealed. There is of course a further resemblance in their creation of characters. Chesterton insisted that Dickens was really a writer of fairy tales, a creator of myths, and this is hardly less true of Balzac. From Pick-wick to the Veneerings, Dickens produced immortals—men more true to themselves than ordinary mortals have time to be—yet hardly one of his women, beyond Mrs. Gamp, is among them. From Madame de Beauséant to Valérie Marneffe, Balzac created immortals, yet Goriot and Hulot are no less. His range was greater than that of Dickens, yet in spite of this and in spite of hostile criticism on his style and construction, Dickens raises less controversy than Balzac. Within certain limits, his status is unchallenged.

There were in the nineteenth century two other writers whose status is unassailed in their own country and in the world, Mark Twain and Gogol. Both were at once exceptional and central, fantastic and serious, humorists who yet embodied deep truths of their lands, as Dickens in England. If Balzac has not the same position in French literature as these three occupy in their own countries, it is largely because his fantastic and comic gifts, his power as a creator of myths, have been diminished by an insis-tence on his realism and his sociological value which, however useful to the historian, may prejudice the liter-ary status of a writer.

Balzac, no less than Mark Twain, Gogol, or Dickens, was not only a fantastic writer, but as with them his fantasy and the play of his imagination were the dominant qualities. Naturally his humour was different from that of these others, as few qualities are so marked both by individual and by national traits. Humour is a matter of temperament, and it is precisely Balzac's temperament that has been obscured by undue concentration on the history and the observation of his work. If his position in literature has been hard to define, it is because this has too often been misjudged.

This problem and the discrepancies between his life and his work are simplified, once he is viewed as a writer of comedy. Even those of his contemporaries who regarded him as a buffoon and caricatured him so often had seen a part of the truth. His own acknowledgment of Rabelais as his master and his devotion to Molière disclosed more. The exuberance of his temperament appeared hardly less in the irony and satire of *La Comédie humaine* than in the humours of the *Contes drolatiques*.

When even so convinced a supporter of his realism as Professor Lukács asserts that Balzac was "the wittiest of writers," it is of interest to ask why there has not been a wider recognition of his comic genius. Emphasis on his romanticism has most obscured this, for the solemnity of the French romantic poets and their rhetoric are often associated with a gravity which excludes humour. Yet it was one of Balzac's characters who first pricked this rhetoric by declaring that Hugo had "only the sensibility of a sublime hall-porter." If Balzac himself sometimes fell into the same rhetoric, he was very different from a Hugo or even a Vigny in their lamentations over the harshness of fate, for it was the whole point of his work from *La Peau de chagrin* onwards that a man's own desires and passions constructed his destiny. This attitude, which was also Molière's, is essentially that of a writer with an eye for comedy, as it sets in relief the foibles and illusions, the postures and impostures of mankind.

That Balzac was at times intoxicated by his own rhetoric proves not that he was a romantic but simply that he was a Frenchman. Another Frenchman, Giraudoux, has noted that the French response to a great occasion is always rhetoric, and he has expressed surprise that the nation of Rabelais and Voltaire should have fallen into a neglect and even fear of satire, which punctures rhetoric. The same change in France has caused a neglect of the strong satirical elements in *La Comédie humaine*, and some have even been too occupied in smiling at Balzac himself to appreciate his comedy. So it has often escaped notice that even his rhetoric is often only an expression of his exuberance, not very different from grandiose claims put forward in his letters to women—the verve is that of a Rabelais, quite distinct from the declamation of a Hugo. It is noteworthy too that his most successful piece for the theatre was the comedy *Mercadet*.

Clearly the comedy of Balzac, based on irony and satire, was very different from the humour of Dickens, but the fact on which he so insisted—that he was writing a history of manners—forced him into comedy, one of whose definitions is the portrayal of manners. Once *La Comédie humaine* is examined with this in mind, it becomes evident how many of the shorter pieces are constructed as comedies. Of the *Scènes de la vie privée* only nine are pure comedies, such as *Un Début dans la vie, Étude de femme*, or *Une fille d'Ève*, but in the others the development is on the lines of comedy, for there is rarely in Balzac the fatality of tragedy. His characters have so much freedom to be themselves that they throw themselves into the arms of death or disaster with hardly less abandon than into the arms of their mistresses.

It is this completeness in their illusions, even when these can only bring misfortune, which to some gives a certain grimness to *La Comédie humaine*. These characters never appeal for pity, as this is not what they want—they know only too well what they want, whether this be love, entry into the salon of Madame de Beauséant, money, a new dress, their neighbours' land, or simply the discovery of the Absolute—but never pity. To a later taste, which sets a high value on "compassion," this may appear hard or even selfish in the refusal to demand a sympathy, now so readily given, for "the human condition." But Balzac's men and women have no quarrel with the human condition, as their energies are all given to quarrels with their husbands, their bankers, their neighbours, or their lovers. For this reason *La Comédie humaine* really is a comedy, not a tragedy, which requires a quarrel with the gods or with the universe.

This is where Balzac is so close to Molière, whose comedies, as that great producer of them, Louis Jouvet, pointed out, all turn on the illusions and fantasies of his characters. It is not only *Le Malade imaginaire* who lives in the imagination, for Alceste is as fantastic in his misanthropy, Harpagon in his avarice.

It is much the same with Balzac, whose Grandet is no less fantastic in his avarice, Birotteau in his dreams of grandeur, Vautrin in his schemes and disguises. Even the purest of his obsessed figures, Balthazar Claes, who pursues nothing less than the Absolute itself, betrays the comic element in his fantasy at the moment when his wife Joséphine bursts into tears at their ruin, and he says: "I have decomposed tears. They contain a little phosphate of lime, sodium chloride, mucus and water."

What is even more remarkable, it is precisely when the scene is most pathetic, when he is achieving what has all the appearances of tragedy, Balzac makes the most devastating use of his genius for comedy. The climax in his two greatest novels, *Le Père Goriot* and *La Cousine Bette*, both bear witness to this.

Goriot's final breakdown and delirium, for all its pathos, abounds in comic touches, as when he reminds God that he too has a son and has an interest in the rights of parents, when he says that he has no wish to die because it will upset his daughters, when finally he mistakes Biachon and Rastignac for them and cries, "My two angels."

So again in *La Cousine Bette*, not content with having made a comedy of the deaths of Valérie and Crevel—her coquetterie with the Almighty, his pompous claim that death will respect a mayor of Paris, the doctor rejoicing in a double autopsy—Balzac goes on to end the book with the grotesque scene of the aged Hulot fumbling with the ugly kitchen wench and being caught by his wife.

It is true that these comic touches heighten the pathos and the horror of these scenes, but it is no less true that the technique is essentially that of comedy, and it is just this which gives the effect of real life, where no moment, however dignified or terrible, can preserve a man or a woman from a sudden lapse into absurdity or the loss of an essential button or tape. In fact, Balzac's realism owes much to his comedy.

If comedy appears less in the *Scènes de la vie de province*, it is never absent and often striking, as in *L'Illustre Gaudissart* and the second part of *Illusions perdues*, which is the finest satire on journalism ever written.

So the *Scènes de la vie parisienne* include the comic misadventures of Nucingen in *Splendeurs et misères des courtisanes*, the demands of La Palferine on his mistress in *Un Prince de la Bohême*, which is almost a *Conte drolatique*, the comedy of *La Cousine Bette*, already discussed, and the last work which Balzac lived to complete, *Le Cousin Pons*, with its wonderful rhapsody on his devotion to his stomach:

> On some days Pons exclaimed, "O Sophie!" thinking of Comte Popinot's cook. A passer-by, hearing this sigh, might have thought he was dreaming of his mistress, but it was something still more precious, a fat carp, garnished with a sauce transparent to the eye, thick on the tongue.

The *Scènes de la vie de campagne* are evidently less in the spirit of comedy, but these four novels are also among the least successful. *Le Médecin de campagne* is more a treatise than a novel, *Le Lys dans la vallée* is of more interest as a tribute to Madame de Berny than as a story, and has faults of "sublimity" which was always Balzac's weakness, as comedy was his strength. *Le Curé de village* has something of both these two, while the fourth, *Les Paysans*, is a favourite only with Professor Lukács, for its economic analysis.

The *Études philosophiques* might be expected to be graver, though they begin with the fantasy of *La Peau de chagrin* and its tribute to Rabelais, while the other pre-ternatural fantasies, such as *L'Élixir de longue vie* and *Melmoth réconcilié*, both receive comic treatment. The horror in stories such as *El Verdugo* or *Adieu* have no comic relief, but they are related to horrors in the *Contes drolatiques*, and arise from a similar exaggeration, the other wing of fantasy. It is only in such mystical works as *Séraphita* and *Louis Lambert* that "sublimity" wholly ousts fantasy, though to some *Séraphita* may seem fantastic enough. While this work is of the first importance to an understanding of Balzac in his conception of human and divine love, a certain heaviness and weakness of construction in it show the strain of a gravity unnatural to him, and explain why some, such as M. Marceau, find it out of place in *La Comédie humaine*.

It is more remarkable that the only *Études analytiques*,

a section where sobriety was to be expected, which Balzac lived to finish, *Physiologie du mariage* and *Petites misères de la vie conjugale*, one of his earliest and one of his latest works, are both witty and humorous pieces, the second being almost farcical in its account of the relations between Caroline and her Adolphe.

This element of comedy in Balzac's work has of course been acknowledged, but it has suffered eclipse by the realist and by the romantic elements, which yet owed their importance to the play of his fantasy, for even his realistic detail, the shape of his houses and of his men's noses, the material of his women's dresses and the colour of their hair, owed everything to the intensity of his hallucination. It is always the fantasists, a Breughel or a Rowlandson, who are most meticulous in their detail.

Balzac has suffered another eclipse, common to the three other writers noted above, Gogol, Mark Twain, and Dickens, who all at some time have been taken too lightly, owing both to their humour and to their popularity. Theirs is a genius which resembles an instinct, a vision which Balzac himself equated with second sight, and it finds a response in a more popular instinct. It is striking that three of these writers began their careers with journalism, while two of them, Dickens and Gogol, had a first ambition to be actors. They were all trained to express themselves in popular terms. Balzac too wanted and achieved popularity, which aroused the envy of writers in his own day, and has confused some judgements of him since. Popular literature may die in a generation, as it becomes literature only in the judgement of many generations, when that first popularity is as dead as those who applauded. Dumas too was a popular writer, and M. Claude Mauriac well expresses the formation of judgement when he speaks of a young man's realisation that Dumas was faulty even at his best, Balzac good even at his worst.

Balzac has survived that first popularity, has survived being dismissed as a romantic, only to be passed over as a realist whose work is "indispensable to the historian." It is true that he is constantly read and recommended in France, that some of the best studies and appreciations of him continue to be written there, but critics remain grudging. If asked who was France's greatest novelist, some might even answer "Balzac, alas," expressing a regret that he was not typical of the French tradition.

If Balzac's reputation today stands higher outside France than among the French, it is for this reason, that he remains a prodigy, an excessive genius, while the qualities most admired by French critics are sobriety and restraint. Conrad, so much influenced by French literature, refers to Balzac as "the Monstrous Shade." Balzac added to the offence of being a prodigy by designing his work with admirable French logic in the *Études* and *Scènes* of *La Comédie humaine*—and then outraging this orderly plan by tumbling into it all the fantasies and humours of his genius, almost as though playing a trick on the Academy which had rejected him.

Yet Rabelais, who more outrageously mocked the Sorbonne, was forgiven in the end, and it is possible than once Balzac is recognised as a fantastic genius of the same order, he too may be pardoned, even by critics in his own country.

To those whose principles and prejudices are different from those of the French, Balzac offers another problem. His fantasies may be appreciated in Germany or Switzerland, in America or in Britain, but those who come to him for the first time may be disconcerted less by his imagination or fantasy than by his darkness—for these characters of *La Comédie humaine* reveal themselves

most often by night, as if they had a real preference for
the dark. It is not only the country doctor who requires
"shadows in the silence," and *Une Ténébreuse affaire* is
only one of many dark doings. It is at night that Rastignac
learns how sinister is Vautrin, how mysterious is Goriot.
At night Raphael perceives the first effects of *La Peau
de chagrin*. At night Grandet counts his gold. At night
Nucingen sees Esther in a clearing of the wood, the
central point of *Splendeurs et misères des courtisanes*
(who are naturally most active at night), and it is at
night that Lucien is arrested. It is at night that Montriveau kidnaps the Duchesse de Langeais, at night that he
finally recovers her corpse from the convent. *Les Chouans*
wage warfare by night, yet the Hulot of *La Cousine
Bette* also campaigns by night until the final skirmish in
the dark attic. Even *L'Envers de l'histoire contemporaine*,
which meditates on works of devotion, opens in dark
corners and stairways. Only *Séraphita* gives an impression
of light . . . set in Norway nearer to the midnight sun.

It is not clear how much this darkness belongs to the
high proportion of journalists, countesses, dandies, courtesans, criminals, and lovers in *La Comédie humaine*,
all of whom are most occupied after dark, how much to
the darkness of the old city of Paris at that period, how
much to the emanation of all from the mind of Balzac
who worked throughout the night. But no frequenter
of *La Comédie humaine* can remain insensible to this
darkness, which some interpret as the grimness of
tragedy.

This is surely to misconstrue what is simply a physical
phenomenon, the falling of night, no more tragic than
a sunset. It is very different from the moral darkness of
Dostoevski, in which men grope for things outside this
world. Balzac's men and women are released by the
coming of the dark to follow their own fantasies, to be
themselves—as are all after the labours of the day—and

the darkness simply gives that sharper relief and sense
of mystery which belongs even to the buildings of the
night. Yet this darkness was uncongenial to the French
mind, which has attached an almost moral value to
clarity, and this again shows that Balzac, like his master
Rabelais, was less a Latin than a Gothic genius.

Yet there is nothing obscure in the desires and motives
of his characters. Even the most impenetrable of them,
Vautrin, is very clear as to what he demands of life. The
women and men of *La Comédie humaine* devote themselves with passion to their human or divine loves, never
resting until they have achieved the object of their
desires. But it is just here that they seem to pass into a
worse darkness, for here so many of them end in death,
Birotteau after the party to celebrate his discharge from
bankruptcy, Claes at the very moment when he thinks
he has discovered the Absolute, Louise Gaston when her
suspicions of her husband have been disproved, Facino
Cane when the Doges' treasure awaits him, Louis
Lambert when he is at last united to his Pauline—and
even Vautrin is cheated of his ambition, for nothing is
more frustrating to a great criminal than to become chief
of police.

These deaths and frustrations, which at first sight
seem to darken the pages of Balzac, are really no different
from the physical darkness, for they too give a sharper
relief and outline to these figures of the night. It is
remarkable how satisfying are Balzac's endings despite
this darkness, while Dickens's "happy endings" are often
disappointing, for it is not easy to believe in Micawber as
an Australian magistrate or even in the geniality of
Scrooge. Dickens, the "indulgent father," could direct
harsh blows at his children, but had to spoil them in the
end, yet they remain immortals because they are in-
capable of change. Because Balzac's men and women
achieve their own destinies and fulfil their own illu-

sions, they reach a different sort of satisfaction, that of
having their own way.

The men of Dickens may appear more fantastic because they pretend more, claiming to be what they are
not, as so many of them from Chadband to Pecksniff or
Podsnap to Skimpole are hypocrites—even the congenial
optimism of a Micawber or a Mark Tapley can only be
taken in "a Pickwickian sense," as a pretence. Yet these
pretences are very human, based on a recognition of
human foibles. Balzac's men and women are not hypocrites; they are terribly and persistently themselves,
never abandoning their obsessions and their desires,
which are their inner substance. It is this implacable
persistence in their identity which makes them fantastic,
this tense and constant exercise of their freedom, their
choice. Most men and women have neither the strength
nor the desire to be themselves at every moment of the
day and night, but relapse into weakness or hypocrisy.
The strain is too much, and a "character" is as rare
as a great man. But in this sense all Balzac's figures are
great men. As Baudelaire noted, even the least of his
characters have genius.

This is why more of Dickens's characters have become
household words, because they represent foibles and
hypocrisies still daily encountered. But the figure of a
Goriot, a Gobseck, or a Vautrin is too great for that—an
ordinary father could no more be compared to a Goriot
than to a King Lear. The scale is too great. It is not only
the duchesses and countesses of Balzac who are not
met in the street, but the de Marsays and the Bianchons,
for the politicians and doctors of real life are more ordinary. In fact the duchesses may be more familiar, for they
have more in them of the feminine which is eternal.

Because the blood of their exuberant creator was in
them, these fantastic creatures could enjoy their freedom,
devoting the same passion to their griefs and losses as

to their joys. Even their deaths are on a par with their
lives, because they are never false. The deaths of Paul
Dombey and little Nell are in every sense unhappy,
because they have been murdered by their father Dickens
to indulge an emotion. Dickens has intervened. Balzac
lets his characters go their own way, and if he intervenes
to comment, it is on their behalf, not on his own.

This freedom of his characters gives an energy, even a
gaiety to his work just at those sombre moments when
Dickens is most depressing. The joys of Dickens are in
his immortals from Pickwick to Sapsea, best preserved
from the real world. But it was in the real world that
Balzac's men and women were most at liberty. This has
given him a reputation for realism, but there was an
important distinction between these men and women
and those of novelists who came after him from Turgenev
or Flaubert to Henry James or Conrad, in none of whom
could the freedom of his fantasy survive. In the language
of modern criticism, all these may be described as better
writers than Balzac, but their men and women were kept
strictly under control. Turgenev's exquisite love stories
could only end sadly, Flaubert's Emma Bovary could
only be frustrated, the Lambert Strether of Henry James
had too fine a conscience for the happiness Maria Gostrey
offered him in Paris, Conrad's Lord Jim had no better
chance. The same doom hung over all of them. They have
the harsh fate of conscripts beside Balzac's volunteers.

Whether the doom was real or literary, whether it was
a change in the world or in the style of novelists, the effect
remains the same on the men and women presented.
Those of Balzac have a unique liberty. If they ruin
themselves, kill themselves, or debauch themselves, it is
by their own choice, not because "life is against them."
Life is what they have inside themselves, their own
vigorous freedom. They are in fact volunteers, because
they act only by their own powerful will—according to

that Treatise on the Will which Louis Lambert had first composed as a boy.

This is the central point in Balzac, this emphasis on the freedom of the will. If his men and women are fantastic or exaggerated, it is because they have this power to be themselves at every moment, at every moment using this freedom which raises them to their seraphic heavens or drives them to their chosen hells. In the history of the novel it is something almost as extraordinary as the appearance of Shakespeare in the history of the drama, and may explain why some consider later novelists with the same qualified approval as is given to dramatists after Shakespeare. For a Goriot is quite as fantastic, if less magnificent, than a Lear. In Balzac, only less than in Shakespeare, an apparent tragedy has all the vitality and exuberance of a comedy.

To some, this energy in Balzac's men and women may appear a shameful lack of discipline, to others, an absurd optimism, but it has something at least of that elemental force which appears in all beginnings, in youth or in the renewal of life at the dawn. It is that primitive desire for expression which leads children and savages to dress up, and it spreads joy over Balzac's darkest pages, because he is obviously enjoying himself, like a child, even more in the horrors than at the parties.

Evidently this is not enough—Balzac also had a powerful intelligence, he had acquired skill as a writer, he corrected incessantly, but that more primitive impulse sometimes showed through even in his most considered pages, and it is on the reaction to this that a judgement on Balzac is usually based. Some critics are shocked by this as others are by nakedness, while some find a childish quality to jar on their sophistication. Later writers have shown a greater art in removing the original source of their inspiration from their work, sometimes to a point where it is possible to doubt whether it ever existed. The gain in smoothness of texture, even in conviction, usually goes with a loss of vitality. If a writer withdraws too much from his work, he may leave it high, but very dry. Balzac's presence in his brings more exasperation than dullness.

To some, exuberance is a quality objectionable in itself. Only those who find it attractive will remain long with Balzac. Others may read, but will not become habitual readers of *La Comédie humaine*, for ultimately its author is less the real—or realistic—Balzac than the Lord R'hoone which was the fantastic anagram he selected for an early work, following his master François Rabelais who signed himself Maistre Alcofribas Nasier.

A fragment left by Balzac at his death, *Une Heure de ma vie*, only recently published, is written by Lord R'hoone in the first person, a man "unfortunately like all others," whose "thoughts and habits have resemblance to those of other men." He considered that an hour of his life "might make a story. . . ." That project was one laid aside, but in every story that he later wrote he was really the first person, because his whole technique was to develop all characters from their own point of view. It is a dramatic technique, and if Lord R'hoone was "like all others," it was as Hazlitt said of Shakespeare that he was like any other man, except that he was like all other men. What the dramatist achieves with the monologue, Balzac did by placing himself inside the character, sharing and expressing his or her tastes and prejudices.

This produced his emphasis on the importance of everything, every detail, every street, every window, every chair, which comes second only to his emphasis on the will. This arises simply because to a man, even more to a woman, no external of dress or home is unimportant. Balzac emphasizes these things not from any belief in the value of realism but from his certainty of their value to the man or woman he is imper-

sonating. He lingered over their furniture or their ornaments because he was, for the moment, touching them
with their hands. The details were important to him
as they are to the child who has to do exactly what
her mother does, exactly what the doctor is seen to
do . . . so was Balzac with Renée de l'Estorade or with
Bianchon.

It is this, much more than any sensation or intrigue,
which creates the vitality of *La Comédie humaine,* for
everything is important as even a shoe is important to
the person who has to wear it. As Balzac wrote of these
things, they also became important to himself. He began
to dress like the dandies he described, to conduct romantic affairs with the countesses of his novels, finally
after all his descriptions of furniture to develop his
bric-à-bracomania, and to prepare a pavillion in the rue
Fortunée for his Polish countess.

Here at last the fantasy and reality merged completely,
for in 1850 he actually married Eveline Hanska, and
seriously ill though he was, they made the terrible journey
from the Ukraine to Paris, which for him, Napoleonic to
the end, was almost as disastrous as the Retreat from
Moscow. But it was not until they reached Paris that
life really showed how Balzacian it could be, for the
manservant left in charge of the splendid house had
gone mad, and when a locksmith opened the door, was
found crouched gibbering in a corner.

Balzac's condition was aggravated by gangrene—he
had grazed his leg against a piece of his beloved furniture—and five months after his marriage he was dead. In
that last joy his *peau de chagrin* had dwindled to
nothing.

He was buried in the cemetery of Père Lachaise,
where Goriot had been put a generation before him.

If life is fantastic, as his certainly was, then *La
Comédie humaine* is a faithful transcription of life. If

life is dull, its truth has to be found in the work of others. Balzac's is at least based on two great requirements of civilisation, the freedom of men to make what they will of their lives, and the importance of everything they touch, everything they believe, everything they love as they hurry on their way towards death.

Note on Sources

Any Balzac bibliography, even the most modest, is not only beyond the limits of an appendix but would fill a book very much longer than this. The great work to consult is:

W. H. Royce. *A Balzac Bibliography*. Chicago. First ed. 1929.

Of works by Balzac's contemporaries, the most useful are the memoirs of his sister Laure de Surville, Lamartine, Gautier, and Hugo's *Choses Vues*.

Below is a short list of works referred to in the text:

Béguin, Albert. *Balzac Visionnaire*. Skira. Geneva. 1946.

Bertault, Philippe. *Balzac. L'Homme et l'œuvre*. Hatier-Boivin. Paris. 1946.

Bouteron, Marcel (ed.). Balzac: *La Comédie humaine*. 10 vols. La Pléiade. N. R. F. Paris. 1935.

Hunt, Herbert J. *Balzac's Comédie humaine*. University of London. 1959.

◄◄◄◄◄◄ INDEX ►►►►►►

INDEX